ENDOR

We are called to live a life of worship, which goes far beyond the twenty minutes we spend singing on Sunday. My friend, Jeff, is an amazing man of God and he lives the life of a true worshiper. In his new book, *Awakening Pure Worship*, you will be challenged to live a lifestyle of worship that will invite the presence of God into all areas of your life.

JOHN BEVERE
Author, Minister
Messenger International

Jeff Deyo lives what he writes. He has modeled a love for God, for people, and a passion to equip the church for over two decades. *Awakening Pure Worship* is an excellent resource to stir your heart toward Jesus as you explore the "why, what, and how" of biblical worship expressed in the modern age. Read it!

PAUL BALOCHE
Worship Pastor, Songwriter

With wit and wisdom Jeff Deyo writes on the "*and*" of worship. Jeff explains how we worship with "spirit *and* truth, skill *and* authenticity, celebration *and* repentance, old *and* new songs," and most importantly that the one we worship is both "King *and* Friend." As a Pentecostal who hungers after both knowledge *and* fire, I appreciate Jeff's holistic approach to worship and the passionate love for Jesus that fuels his living. As a conservative who loves the theology found in many old hymns, I appreciate how Jeff respects the ancient truths *and* the new mediums. As a worshiper, I appreciate how Jeff affirms both the reverence *and* joy with which we approach Jehovah. Jeff's thoughts will indeed awaken us to what is pure about worship. What he writes about is not complicated, it's just hard—but in that challenge there is incredible beauty and fulfillment. In pure worship, we both give *and* receive.

DICK BROGDEN, PHD.
Founder of the Live Dead Movement
Cairo, Egypt

By the grace of God, I have had the opportunity to know and walk with many people of influence. I have had the honor of ministering behind the scenes and impacting the lives of some of these "movers and gatherers." After I had moved to Nashville, Tennessee, I heard about a young worship leader who was hosting Worship City Praise events every month from church to church across the region. I jumped in the middle of the pile and eventually became one of this dear man's cheerleaders! He shook the rafters with his vibrant vocals and capacity to direct people to the One! His name is none other than Jeff Deyo. Whether it was the heights of Sonicflood, establishing the Pure Worship Institute, or being a professor at North Central University in Minneapolis, Minnesota, this man has lived his music and his worship. I highly commend to you the life, the music, and now the writings of my friend, Jeff Deyo. Why? It's like he wears a street sign over his chest with an arrow pointing upward that states, "Look up!" Thank you, Jeff, for composing and living *Awakening Pure Worship*.

JAMES W. GOLL
Founder of God Encounters Ministries
Author, Communications Trainer, Consultant

Jeff Deyo understands the heart this generation has for authentic and primal faith. He provides a clarion call to come before God, with all we are, and dare to believe we can know Him intimately, personally, and recklessly. As a songwriter, author, and worship leader, Jeff is an industry expert. Even more so, as a worshiper himself Jeff speaks from experience and vulnerability to create a hunger deep within the reader to know God more.

HEATH ADAMSON
Author, *Grace in the Valley*
Chief of Staff, Convoy of Hope
Global Chairman, World Assemblies of God Fellowship Next Gen

Jeff Deyo's new book, *Awakening Pure Worship*, is a must read for worship leaders and worshipers alike. It is the culmination of years of disciplined musical development, proven experience in the practical world of local church and national leadership conferences, along with the academic setting of the university classroom. Jeff's work is biblically based, theologically sound, and reflects the depth of his own spiritual life. It's the most insightful writing on worship I've seen. It really is a must read.

GORDON ANDERSON, PH.D
Former President, North Central University

Jeff (however you pronounce his last name) has been a friend and mentor for many years. What he talks about in the pages of this book is none other than pure gold forged. The kind of metal, value, that only arises from the process of a life that has been awakened from the ashes. Who Jeff is off the stage, with real people in real places, makes this not just a book to read, but a voice to be heard.

ERIC SAMUEL TIMM
Orator, Author, Artist, Visionary
EricSamuelTimm.com
TheAxeAcademy.com
PaintingHope.com
C4Orators.com

In a highly readable book, Jeff Deyo (I know that name; he's written worship songs) invites us to join him on his journey of discovery—what worship is and isn't. He does it in a conversational style that is winsome and upbeat. He is probing issues we have had with worship—the what, why, who, and how. He answers our questions, and sometimes questions our answers—in a personal rather than preachy tone, invitational and humble. Jeff is not a know-it-all—though he's a professor of worship—but he's definitely a discover-it-all. I like the layout. It is easy to know where Jeff is going. His style will appeal to young adults—of all ages. It is reader friendly for both evangelicals and charismatics.

PAUL ANDERSON
Pastor, Author
The Master's Institute, Founder

Finally, a book on worship by Jeff Deyo! Jeff Deyo's new book, *Awakening Pure Worship*, draws from his experience from his role as the front man for Sonicflood to his present role as worship arts professor at North Central University. Jeff wonderfully guides the reader on a relaxed and personal journey into a greater understanding of this beautiful thing we call worship. A bridge builder by nature, Jeff invites us to cross over into new ways to look at and experience a life of worship. You'll feel like you're sitting right there next to him as he unveils one magnificent nugget after another. I highly recommend this book for everyone, from the casual singer to the die-hard worshiper. *Awakening Pure Worship* is a delight!

CHRIS DuPRÉ
Pastor, Speaker, Songwriter
Author of *The Wild Love of God*

Jeff Deyo is putting words to his soul with this call for resurrecting the life-blood of the church. We need a guide to navigate the terrain of time and resources being dedicated to worship, and Jeff is that guide.

JARED ANDERSON
Singer, Songwriter
A pack mule for the Master of Imagination

Lots of people have written books on worship. Jeff Deyo has lived a life of worship. Both on and off the stage, his life and ministry serve as shining examples of what *Awakening Pure Worship* really looks like. As his home church pastor, I highly recommend this book not only for those who lead others in song, but for anyone desiring to experience the presence of God every day of their life.

DERRICK ROSS
Lead Pastor, Celebration Church
Lakeville, Minnesota

I have known Jeff Deyo for many years—from Sonicflood to his time as a professor at my alma mater, North Central University. Throughout our long friendship, I have always known that Jeff is a true worshiper, which is why his heart of worship is so very contagious. Every person needs to hear Jesus' call to a transformational relationship with Him. Throughout the pages of this book, Jeff shares profound and practical insights into the reasons why we worship, the One whom we worship, and how worship can be an authentic way to respond to God's grace from a place of honesty and brokenness. From the worship leader to the guy sitting on the back row, I highly recommend this book.

REGGIE DABBS
Motivational Speaker, Author, Musician, Friend

As I was reading *Awakening Pure Worship*, I had the sense that I was sipping coffee with Jeff and having a conversation about worship with him. His heart and thoughts are clearly communicated in a way that is both relevant and timeless. As a worship leader in my 25th year of ministry, I have learned *so* much from Jeff and I am excited for many generations to glean from his wisdom, compelling them to worship with fervor and authenticity until we truly experience the reality of *on earth as it is in heaven!*

JAYE THOMAS
Singer, Songwriter, Recording Artist
Worship Leader, International House of Prayer Kansas City
Director, Forerunner School of Worship (IHOPU)

Jeff Deyo is one of those down-to-earth, refreshing guys. His heart for Jesus is real. And his fascinating stories will cause you to think, "Wow, we truly have a crazy opportunity to worship God." His book does a fantastic job of deconstructing many of the modern ways we cripple authentic worship. Yet, it's uplifting. He writes as though you're going on a walk. This book will truly cause you to break out of your preconceived notions of worship into a fresh encounter with God. It's a perfect book to take your walk with Christ to a new level. I'm so glad I took the time to read it.

PETER HAAS
Lead Pastor, Substance Church, Minneapolis, Minnesota
Author of *Pharisectomy: How to Remove Your Inner Pharisee and other Religiously Transmitted Diseases*
Producer / Electronic Dance Music D.J. for SubstanceVariant.com

As one of the leading voices in the worship community, Jeff Deyo has not only learned about worship, he has lived it. This book is filled with life lessons from God's heart. There is so much more to worship than the songs we sing, and God has given Jeff an incredible revelation of what it truly means to worship God in spirit and in truth.

JONATHAN LEE
Songwriter, Worship Leader
Worship Pastor, Cedar Rapids First Assembly

Jeff Deyo is first and foremost a proven and faithful worshiper. He's cultivated his love affair with Jesus for over four decades. As President of North Central University, I have had a front-row seat when it comes to experiencing his voice and leadership. Not only is Jeff's music and worship second to none, his teaching and seasoned maturity is exactly what this next generation of worshipers needs. His new book, *Awakening Pure Worship*, is a beautifully written convergence of his personal and professional worship life. Once you read it, I promise you'll quickly get copies for the people you care about.

SCOTT HAGAN
President, North Central University

The content captured within these pages brings such a relevant and sincere approach to worship. Jeff's foundation is completely built upon his relationship with Jesus, and this is fully evident in the way he pours out his heart in each and every chapter. This book is for anyone ready to go deeper in their pursuit of God's presence.

DANIEL ERIC GROVES
Teaching Pastor, Worship Artist
Relentless Church, Greenville, SC

We have ten thousand worship leaders but few worship fathers. Jeff carries the heart of a true father and shepherd that will jump off these pages as he speaks honestly to worshipers, worship leaders, and worship musicians. Thank you, Jeff Deyo, for leading us so well.

JON EGAN
Executive Worship Pastor
New Life Church

AWAKENING

PURE

CULTIVATING A
CLOSER FRIENDSHIP
WITH GOD

WORSHIP

JEFF DEYO

DESTINY IMAGE® PUBLISHERS, INC.

P.O. Box 310, Shippensburg, PA 17257-0310

"Promoting Inspired Lives."

This book and all other Destiny Image and Destiny Image Fiction books are available at Christian bookstores and distributors worldwide.

Cover design by Eileen Rockwell

Interior design by Terry Clifton

For more information on foreign distributors, call 717-532-3040.

Reach us on the Internet: www.destinyimage.com.

ISBN 13 TP: 978-0-7684-4286-1

ISBN 13 eBook: 978-0-7684-4287-8

ISBN 13 HC: 978-0-7684-4289-2

ISBN 13 LP: 978-0-7684-4288-5

For Worldwide Distribution, Printed in the U.S.A.

1 2 3 4 5 6 7 8 / 22 21 20 19 18

DEDICATION

I DEDICATE THESE writings—my first full book—to my faithful wife, Martha, and to my sweet children, Roman, Evan, Channing, and Clara. My prayer is that each of you would engage passionately on the incredible life journey of awakening pure and intimate fellowship with your Father in heaven until—and beyond—that beautiful day when we literally see our Lord Jesus face to face. I also pray that your hunger for deep relationship would spill over into your friendships with many, many family members and friends as you generously share your awakened love for God with people all over the world. I love you and am incredibly thankful to be doing life with such an amazing, Spirit-filled clan.

Special thanks goes out to David Sluka who supported, encouraged, and helped me greatly in the early stages of these writings, to James Goll, a spiritual father and friend who has cheered me on for many years now, to the unparalleled students at North Central University who grant me the joy of pouring into them and learning from them, and to my Celebration Church family, who has walked closely with us through thick and thin. You all have a special place in my heart as well as a significant part in this book. Thank you all.

CONTENTS

FOREWORD

JEFF DEYO IS the real deal. For him, the movements of the heart are
more important than the reasoning of the mind. Relationship with
God trumps religious rules. If it's not God-breathed and God-in-
spired, it's not a consideration. Jeff is a man of the Word and the Spirit
who longs for authentic, wholehearted intimacy with Jesus.

I'm honored to call him my friend.

Awakening is not an incidental word in a title, but it is this book's
essential message. First, Jeff tells of his own awakening to true worship, especially during his years with Sonicflood. Then, he points the
way to *your* awakening. He puts down markers in this book that, if
followed, will awaken your heart to the thrill of intimate communion
with your Lord and Savior, Jesus Christ.

There *is* an awakening to worship. It's possible to groove with
the music and enjoy the delight of singing with throngs of believers
but still not be awakened to true worship. The awakening of which
I speak is a work of the Holy Spirit. It often comes in a moment of
time, in an encounter with Jesus that becomes unforgettable.

I had such a moment, such an altar. I can tell you where I stood,
in 1982, in Detroit, Michigan. I experienced Jesus in corporate worship like never before. The spark of the experience ignited my heart.
Something was imprinted on my spirit. I was marked. Ruined. Never
again could I return to the staid formalism of my past experience. I
had to go forward. Even though I didn't always pursue Him with

perfect wisdom, my heart was awakened for more of Him and nothing was ever again the same.

Something like that happened to Jeff, too. You're going to read about it in this book. And a similar God encounter can happen for you. Perhaps that's why this book has come into your hands. For such a time as this.

I pray God uses this book as a tool in your own awakening. May your heart be marked with an insatiable desire for intimacy with Jesus that is true, spiritual, real, vibrant, and radiantly pure. May you be ruined for more of Him!

Bob Sorge
Kansas City, Missouri
February, 2018

INTRODUCTION

YOU'VE WONDERED, HAVEN'T you? Wondered if it was really possible to cultivate that one-on-one, deeper-than-deep, BFF-type relationship with God so many leaders, preachers, and authors talk about. Of course, like me, you're a follower of Christ. Or maybe not. Maybe you're not entirely sure. Regardless, you've wrestled with this intimacy with God idea. Too many times it hasn't been a reality in your own life. A *real* reality. At least not to the degree you desire. Not in the way *they* talk about it.

If you're honest, it's a real battle. Life is hard, and God seems far away. Juggling normal life priorities can be overwhelming. Managing relationships with family and friends seems next to impossible. Let alone maintaining a potent relationship with God. Let's be real. You're not even sure you like using the word *intimacy* in connection with God. And it does occasionally irk you when people say things like, "And the other day God told me...." You wonder if He *really* told them or if they're just being, you know, leaderish.

Been there.

Then again, maybe you're different. Maybe those people have something you don't. Or need something you don't. Maybe they're making it up? Or faking it up?

I've wondered too.

Sure, it's possible you've simply closed yourself off to God in ways that are just too convoluted to reopen. Maybe you're too deep in sin, or just too busy doing ministry. Come on, let's face it. You could never really be *that* close with God. Like Moses—where you walk and talk with Him *face to face?* That's for spiritual giants. Truth be told, it feels like your prayers bounce regularly off the ceiling. Unanswered, mostly.

Corporate worship songs are nice, but sometimes they seem to function more as a to-do item in a church service order or perhaps something we do to cultivate "community" instead of something designed to help us nurture our real-time, personal connection with God.

Sometimes church seems to be more about entertainment—listening in on talented speakers and gifted musicians. Or about a social club—where we eat good food, sing nice songs, and hang out in our own little religious bubble. Other times it seems to be mostly about finding ways to reach the marginalized, the lost, and the poor. Which certainly isn't bad. At all. Yet, you were hoping it was possibly, maybe, hopefully going to involve you growing a little bit—or even a lot a bit—in your life with God? Could be. Not sure. Maybe that's not the point at all. But, could there be more to church? To God? To singing? To worship? Could I actually come to know God? As a close friend? As a true Father? As a true King? To be with Him every day? In a way that isn't about crossing off the "religious duty" item on my checklist?

That's what this book is about.

It's for Christians as well as for people who are searching. Honestly, it's more of a conversation than a book. As you read it, it'll be like we're hanging out talking about worship, about life, and about the deep things of God.

I'm a little odd. I'm a thinker *and* a feeler, and I like to dive multiple layers down into God, into all that He is. To talk about Him. To think about Him. To meditate on His Word. To investigate Him. To be with Him. To taste and see. Him.

My heart hurts. There is so much pain in this world. Maybe in your world. I personally know so many people whose lives have been turned upside down by tragedy, circumstances, or poor choices. It rocks me. The enemy is so tactical in the way he distracts, detracts, and attracts. He'll do anything to keep us from our one true purpose. From true awakened worship. And to keep us from pure freedom, pure joy, and pure life—those things that arise as a result of unadulterated communion with God.

It's like relationship with God is unleaded gasoline, and the enemy is tempting us with diesel and 789 other types of fluids that make it impossible for a car designed specifically for unleaded gasoline to run smoothly. If at all.

I've realized it's a fight. For me, personally. For my family. And for you. That's why I'm compelled to share these writings. They've been burning in my heart for 25 years. I'm driven to do my part. To stand for you and your family. God is calling us each into greater fellowship with Him, and maybe—just maybe—my simple deliberations in this book can serve as a lifeline of encouragement for you and for those you love.

One of the interesting ways I communicate my heart for worship in this book is to share my own life journey of how God has been awakening pure worship in me since my early Sonicflood days. How He took this little conservative, evangelical kid and filled him with a passion for tangible, deeper friendship with his heavenly Father— something many of us desperately hope is possible, yet all too often escapes us.

The ideas and strategies in this book are going to help you rekindle your lost hope once again—the hope *and* the means—along with every individual on the planet—to entertain an authentic, personal connection with God. A growing connection. A passionate connection. A daily connection. I know if He can do this work in me, He will do it in you.

Is it really possible to walk and talk with our Father God in the power of the Holy Spirit? In the supernatural? Overcoming the trials, the troubles, and the temptations of this world? Or is it simply an illusory idea for those who need to feed their crutch or for those who can't seem to dream of surviving in this ferocious existence called life?

You want to believe God is with you. You want to believe He is as real and as accessible as people say. You want to invite Him into your Sunday services, into your family interactions, into your everyday workday. But how?

It seems like we exist on two different planets. One where we pray and sing and read the Bible—in church. In small groups. Around holidays. And another where we struggle through the challenges of everyday, real life—at work and with our family. These two planets seem worlds apart—that is, except when we manage to put on our religious face and attempt to pray before a meal or at bedtime with our kids.

Here's the thing.

I'm convinced we've got a lot of it backwards. Worship is not an obligation. It is an invitation. It's not a church service. It's an adventure. Not so much toward God, but *with* God.

Relationship with God doesn't culminate with Jesus on the cross. Or even with His resurrection. That's just the beginning. Not the end. It doesn't end with heaven or with harps in our hands. It ends with concrete, supernatural hang-time with the Creator of the universe. For all eternity.

Awakened worship isn't about songs or goose bumps. It's not about church growth or Sundays. It's not about trendy choruses or time-tested hymns. It's about love. It's about friendship. With God.

You see, there are generally three types of people:

- Those who've given up on encountering God. They believe they'll never be spiritual enough, and they imagine this God-thing is only for special people or big-time leaders. Or they've decided it's all a hoax.

- Those who have been deceived into believing they already have an intimate connection with God, yet they don't. This is scary. Either they've danced just outside the circle of relationship with Him, or they've unknowingly enjoyed religion, good deeds, atmospheric church services, and charismatic people instead of God Himself.

- Those who have truly encountered God deeply and personally and who are on the fast track toward powerful, daily, ever-more-vibrant relationship with the Lover of their soul.

Where do you sit? Where do I?

Seems to me, the Bible makes it clear that this type of deep, personal, intimate relationship with God is something He desires—and expects—and anticipates. For every person. From every person.

But how does it come about?

In this book, we'll discuss—in four sections—the *what, why, who,* and *how* of worship. Of relationship:

- What: Sometimes words need a refresher when their meaning gets diluted. What exactly is worship? The few minutes of singing before the sermon? Serving the least of these? Time in the secret place? A combination? Here, we will explore as much of what worship is *not*— via the story of God awakening pure worship in me—in order to refocus our understanding on what exactly pure worship is.

- Why: I share many personal stories in this book—things I've learned and am still learning through the Holy Spirit and from other incredible followers of Christ. What's the point of worship, anyway? Is it for God? Is it for me? What are the reasons I should engage? How important is it really? What, if any, are the benefits and immediate incentives for us to go beyond a "surface" religion?

- Who: Red flag alert! If we get the *what, why,* and *how* parts of worship right, yet fail to get the *who* part right, we're in serious trouble. Who is the Father? Who is Jesus? Who is the Holy Spirit? Really? Clearly, the other elements we cover become impotent if we apply them to the wrong god. A false god. For this reason, I spend considerable time highlighting the importance of understanding *who* we worship as well as the all-too-prevalent dangers of worshiping a god we've created in *our* image.

- How: We take a zoomed-in look into how we can flourish as a pure worshiper. What are the characteristics of these folks, and how do they become awakened worshipers? What action steps do they take in moving from wishing they were pure worshipers to actually becoming pure worshipers? It is shocking just how much our modern-day "worshipers" tend to resemble Pharisees rather than true worshipers.

In the end, my great desire is to guide you and those you love into discovering God—either again, or for the first time. Or at least to deeper levels than ever before—together in tangible, everyday ways.

It's true. God is meant to be our constant companion. The one we speak with in two-way conversation constantly—both *in* the secret place *and* throughout the day. His Spirit is actually meant to empower us constantly and involve us continually in supernatural encounters, moment by moment. Our journey with God—this side of heaven—is meant to be a wonderful yet incomplete precursor or teaser for all that we will experience when we finally graduate into literal, *face-to-face* relationship with God in eternity. All creation is groaning for that great day. But even now the stage is set. For relationship. For friendship. For fellowship. For love. Between a powerful, omnipotent God and His beloved creation.

So, if you've found yourself discouraged or dry or lost on developing an engaging, walking-and-talking relationship with God, let's talk. Jump in with me on the journey. The one where God awakens, or reawakens, pure worship in you and in me.

SECTION 1

WHAT IN THE WORLD IS WORSHIP?

CHAPTER 1

UNEARTHING MUSICAL WORSHIP

"We are called to an everlasting preoccupation with God."
—A.W. TOZER

I SAT. FIDGETING in church, as usual. Thirteen years old. Singing the same old songs. Again. Two standing up and two sitting down. In pews. From a red, hardbound book. Stanzas one, two, and four. Never three.

I grew up in church. It's what I knew. It was honestly a fairly enjoyable part of my life. But I didn't understand that I didn't understand worship. Musical worship, that is.

One of our church board members stood passively on the platform keeping everyone on the same page, keeping everyone in time, keeping everyone in line. Conducting. I wasn't bothered by it. Nor was I moved by it. It was just what we did. Each week.

Singing. Why did we do it? I wondered passingly.

A way to remember truth? A way to share inspiring works of art? A way to absorb the Gospel? A way to assemble theology? A way to enjoy camaraderie and emphasize community? A way to carry on our traditions?

Too much for me to worry about.

Don't get me wrong, I get it now. The words of the hymns I grew up with *were* and *are* invigorating. Grandiose. Thought-provoking. For many, they are life-changing. But for me, at 13, they were just plain hard to relate to. Like snow showers in summer. The lyrics didn't fit my vocabulary. Almost like Japanese. A language I didn't speak in the schoolyard or the backyard. One I still don't speak in normal conversation.

You know, the thees, and thous, and the heretos, and wherefore arts? And, of course, the Yoda talk. A language from a galaxy far, far away, we did sing.

Old English.

I enjoyed music tremendously and loved God passionately, but the songs—with their alien language—created a sort of barrier for me. And I don't think I was the only one.

No doubt. These were the mantras of a generation come and almost gone. A passionate generation, mind you. But one of a different era. Their anthems were absolutely birthed out of great struggle and earnest pursuit of God. A cry of devotion that spoke of rock solid, fervent followers of Christ, determined to sing out—and live out— their theology while celebrating their steadfast love for God via the prevailing sounds of their time. As they should.

Even so, I was going to need more if this was going to become more for me.

I wrestled with their expressions. I wrestled with their melody stylings and lyrical phrasing. Attempting to comprehend. Yet feeling disconnected.

The heart was there, but I had trouble embracing these works of art as my own. I appreciated them. Truly. But relating to them was a different story. A thought skipped through my mind. Just as these godly hymn writers had poured out passionate praises from their day, I needed—we needed—to be able to discover God for ourselves and then bring forth our own expressions. New and different.

Yet grounded in the same ancient truths and penetrating presence encountered by our parents and grandparents. Desiring to set our hopes anew on God, for our generation, in the same way generations before us had done.

Clearly, they didn't blindly embrace the songs and sounds of a generation before them, but they composed majestic refrains of their own, spawned from their own encounters with God. Fresh. Real. Profound. Personal.

Truth is, if I was expected to connect with God relationally while singing these lyrics together with these timeworn melodies, yeah, I missed the memo. Mostly because the language kept me from deciphering the message. But also for this reason—I never quite understood the ultimate purpose. Of worship. Of singing in church. Of regurgitating songs with which I struggled to resonate.

Still, I never thought to ask.

HEART AWAKENED

I gave my heart to God when I was four years old. I might as well have been born in a pew. Mainstream, evangelical church. My dad led me to the Lord one ordinary night by my bedside. Knees bent. Hands folded. Heart awakened. I receive Jesus as my Lord and Savior, and I've been growing to love Him and serve Him more and more ever since.

Interestingly, I've been cultivating a love for His Church more and more ever since as well. Yet one of the things that strongly hindered me was my inability to make the critical connection between an increasing relationship with God and musical worship. Singing. A truly *personal*, intimate relationship with God expressed through song.

I missed it completely.

You see, when I was growing up, we often utilized the word *personal* to describe our relationship with God. The very idea of Christianity dictated relationship over religion. And we clarified this regularly. But I don't think I understood what it meant back then—at least not as I do today. And I really don't think many folks around me did either.

I grew up in an amazing family. I regularly read my Bible and prayed in solitude in my room, starting in middle school. I specifically sought wisdom, knowledge, and understanding as I read daily from Psalms and Proverbs and other books of the Bible. I truly wanted to understand God, to obey God. I often asked Him for help when I had problems. I didn't dislike church gatherings. And I loved youth group. I wanted to follow Jesus. I enjoyed music and didn't dislike singing hymns. Even so, the thought simply never occurred to me that I could or should attempt to pursue a close friendship with God—or that this friendship could be amped up through singing. For Him. About Him. To Him.

Intimacy with God? Friendship with God? These were fairly foreign terms. Fairly odd too. Plus, it seemed like maybe God was too big, too busy, or too far away for all this. From my vantage point. Let me clarify. No one told me this. But few told me otherwise, that I remember.

I assumed real fellowship with God was something for pastors and leaders only. I never imagined God was equally, truly available to me.

Church mostly seemed like something we attended to keep us on the straight and narrow. To keep us from falling prey to the devil. Which was good. Yet I never really considered that we might expect to walk and talk with God like Adam and Eve or like Moses. And I certainly never imagined this could be spurred on as I lifted my heart to Him in song—in a church service or in my bedroom. Of course, like many, I assumed singing was something we only did at church or in concert halls. And I assumed real fellowship with God was something for pastors and leaders only. I never imagined God was equally, truly available to me.

To me, singing was horizontal, not vertical. We had more of a song service than a worship service. We were being led by a song leader, more than a worship leader. We sang theologically profound songs with great historical significance. Eternal truths that depicted a glorious, foundational, Kingdom vision for life. Yet this was a vision to be understood more than encountered. It was more about a service than it was about a person. More cerebral than spiritual. Not that I even understood these concepts at 13. I was oblivious, I guess. Young. Learning. Simply receiving what others taught me. Or receiving only what I was perceiving. I don't know. Maybe no one ever suggested anything different, or maybe I just wasn't listening. Maybe a bit of both.

Regardless, singing seemed like an end to me, not a means. We sang God's truth. Together. No doubt, the songs endeavored to shape my thinking. Truly. And the potential was all there. If we let them. If we were fortunate. If we could break through the thousand-foot-thick cultural walls.

But then it was lunchtime, and we went home.

Nevertheless, there was something in me—tugging—something that kept burning, suggesting there was more to God. Something more to church. Something more to worship. Much, much more.

MUSIC IN MY BLOOD

I loved music. I took piano lessons. I played drums. I sang and wrote songs.

My parents were both musical. They met at Taylor University where my mom majored in voice and my dad played in a tremendous traveling trombone trio. (Oh, if only YouTube existed back then!) My sister pursued a music performance degree in flute at Wheaton College while I had the incredible privilege of enrolling in a special class at Lawrence North High School in Indianapolis, Indiana called Music Careers. I ate, drank, and slept music. I was nearly voted "Best

Musician" in my senior class, but for Benji what's-his-name, a talented guitarist with long hair and leather pants. #soclose #notbitter.

I was drum line captain in our very competitive Indiana high school marching band for two years. I was the animated keyboardist in my very first Christian rock band in tenth grade called 717 (based on a Bible verse, to be sure, but for the life of me, I can't remember which one). I was having a blast. Music ran through my veins. But I had no idea what worship was. Absolutely no idea.

I found myself sitting for hours at our little upright piano with my Sony duel-cassette recorder enthusiastically picking out Genesis and Chicago tunes note by note. The white keys were all jaggedly chipped at the ends as a result of either my sister or me hammering them with wooden blocks as a toddler. (We never did discover the culprit.) Yet I remained undaunted in my musical pursuits.

Play. Pause. Find it on the piano. Rewind. Play. Pause. Find it on the piano. Rewind. Play. Pause. Find it on the piano. Rewind. Over and over again.

Hours of delight. Hours.

I remember writing one of my first "Christian" songs straight out of Proverbs 3:25-26. It was about overcoming fear. *"You need not be afraid of sudden disaster or the destruction that comes upon the wicked, for the Lord is your security. He will keep your foot from being caught in a trap."* Scripture songs. Straight from the Bible. Why not? Straight from the source. (Plus, it's the only place you can lift lyrics and not be accused of plagiarism, right?)

In those days, God was giving me an increasing heart for His Word and for my peers. I wanted nothing more than to connect my three loves—God, people, and music. I saw music as a fun, yet potent, way to share the message of Jesus with those who were misguided by a love for temporary worldly pleasures. Those hurting from the pains of life. Those broken by life's daunting circumstances. Those offended by hurtful, harmful people. And it certainly was. But I couldn't tell you much about this thing called worship.

Don't you know, at that time, my youth group sang songs like "Pharaoh, Pharaoh" and "Lean on Me" for "worship"? We even had hand motions for the songs. In high school, no less! We didn't think anything of it. We didn't know any different. What we had was good. We just didn't know there was more.

I'm actually quite thankful for my journey, yet I also recognize my undeniable ignorance toward what I've grown to know today as worship.

MADE FOR THE STAGE

All through high school and college I wrote, recorded, and performed songs. Christian songs. Passionate songs. Scriptural songs. Good songs. God songs. But not worship songs. At least not worship songs in the way we currently define them. That is, not corporate in nature. Not songs we would sing together as a church body, but songs people would primarily listen to and enjoy as someone else sang them on stage—concert style.

I remember attending a Michael W. Smith/dc Talk concert in the spring of 1991 and thinking to myself, "I was born for this. I was created to do music on a stage like that." I could feel it as I peered across the vast crowd to the tiny performers on the other side of the oval-shaped arena. Like it was my destiny. At least a version of it.

After graduating from Anderson University in 1992 with a Music Business degree and marrying my sweet Martha, we spent eight months ministering with Youth For Christ in Singapore. Then we moved to Nashville in the spring of 1993. To follow my musical dreams. The dreams I believed with all my heart were from the Lord. Like many though, I was truly ignorant of the process involved in beginning a music ministry. I believed a beautiful fantasy—that I'd have a major record contract, a brand-new album in stores, a chart-topping single, and a Prevost tour bus rolling down the road, all in six months' time.

Yep. Can you say, naive?

I recorded three independent CDs, played whatever dates I could find, hired an artist manager, all the while playing showcases and trying to drum up support for my Christian hip hop career.

Uh huh. You heard that right. Hip hop.

If only this were a picture book. But you have your imagination.

I raised some money, purchased a conversion van, bought a sound and lighting system, and set out on the road with my soundtracks and my dance moves. All in hopes of changing the world for Jesus.

And you can be sure I did. But the world also changed me.

I found myself losing hope after about four years of trying to "make it." Without a record deal in sight. Playing shows for $50—or just for a meal and a couch to sleep on—wasn't cutting it. Sure glad my resourceful wife, Martha, was back home working a *real job* as an administrator for an accounting firm to hold down the fort. (I guess we'd call her a sugar momma—the wife of a starving musician who actually has a decent job and can pay the bills so her artist husband can continue to pursue the big dream.)

I loved students. I loved music. I loved ministry. And I loved writing songs that challenged and encouraged people. I wrote a rap called "True Love Awaits" about waiting for sex, based on the '90s True Love Waits campaign. I penned a song called "Eyez on Him" about hypocrisy and the televangelist world—complete with a hijacked audio sample from the Top 40 hit song "Everybody Dance Now" (before this was illegal, of course). I even had a song inspired by DJ Jazzy Jeff and the Fresh Prince's "Parents Just Don't Understand" called "Drinkin's Outa Hand." I was all about it! And it was all good.

But I definitely didn't know much about musical, corporate worship.

EYEZ TOWARD HEAVEN

All this began to change in 1997 when I signed on as the lead singer of Gotee Records' surfer rock band, Zilch. Zilch was made up mostly of band members from the popular Christian mega-band, dc Talk.

We toured when they weren't touring. (Big shout out to TobyMac, CEO of Gotee, as well as president, Joey Elwood, for believing in us.)

We definitely weren't a worship band, and we weren't generally that successful either. But after a few months, we did recognize a growing trend of many popular Christian bands to add a couple worship songs to the end of their set. In response, we worked up a Radio Head-esque version of the classic chorus, "Lord, I Lift Your Name on High" and started rocking it as our closing song in the set each night.

It was our little nod to God. A way to jump on the Christian worship band bandwagon. An attempt to prove to youth pastors everywhere that we were focused on ministry and not just on our careers.

But then something happened.

People started responding. Genuinely. Deeply. All while we played that little unassuming worship song at the tail end of our set. A song that honestly struck me as painfully cheesy in earlier years.

It scared me. I mean, I was brought up in a good conservative church—you know, the kind where if someone raised their hand, we assumed they had a question. But now people were raising their hands and running to the altar. Without invitation. And this little church boy was freaking out, because that just wasn't the way we did things.

They were kneeling and crying. Tears of repentance and joy ran down their faces. They sang with all of their hearts. They lifted up holy hands. They wouldn't be silenced. We had unknowingly struck a nerve. It was as if this "new" worship had suddenly burst a dam that had been frantically holding back people's passion for Jesus. For years. It was no joke. We were seeing something we had never seen before. Many people seemed to be turning their eyes toward heaven, turning their eyes toward Jesus, turning their eyes toward eternal things…and away from us. Huh? Away from us?

Wait.

That's not good. Is it? We're trying to build a brand here. Trying to establish a name for ourselves. Trying to get noticed. This can't be right. We're…

Oh, never mind. Scratch that. Who cares.

It was indisputable. It was overwhelming. It was beautiful. It was what we always wanted.

In light of all this new God-awareness, nobody really seemed to care about brand awareness. We knew one thing. The more we sang that song, the more we wanted to sing that song. Because the more we sang that song, together, in that moment, the more we seemed to enjoy God—all of us—for real. Somehow, of course, we knew it wasn't the song itself. It was so much more than that. It was God moving in the expression of that song as we lifted our hungry praise to Him in a childlike freedom that silenced the naysayers.

No doubt. God was filling those moments like crazy, highlighting them so we could experience something we'd all been longing to experience but that had always, so often, eluded us in the past. True ministry. True connection. True encounter. True worship.

As we lifted Him up—as we cried out to God—He was seriously, undeniably drawing people closer to Himself. By the boatloads. You could feel it. You could taste it. We saw it happening with our own eyes! The atmosphere was rich with God. Not of religion or Christian clichés. Not of man-made hype or emotion. Not of skilled entertainers having their way with a gullible crowd. No. We were experiencing something special. Undeniable. We were beginning to lose ourselves. And yet we were gaining Him. Like never before.

CHAPTER 2

INTIMACY BEFORE MINISTRY

"For years, the church has emphasized evangelism, teaching, fellowship, missions, and service to society to the neglect of the very source of its power—worship."
—ROBERT E. WEBBER

FUNNY THING IS, we hadn't anticipated it. Yet it hit us like a mighty humpbacked whale splashing down into the sea after an impressive leap. God was doing something we were completely unprepared for—pulling *us* closer to Him. Even as we led hungry Zilch concert-goers to connect with God, we were being drawn to Him as well. Who knew? We never saw it coming. God was now moving in *us*? What? We were the artists. We were trying to help the audience. The ticketholders. You know, we were on a mission. There for them. Doing ministry. For the poor, lowly, needy people.

Ironically, we never imagined God might want to move powerfully in *our* lives in the process. The poor, lowly, needy artists who couldn't even see their own need. Truth is, we had seriously overlooked our own profound hunger for deeper fellowship with God. Or at least the notion that we too required a continual refreshing touch from Him.

We had inadvertently done what so many do. We had positioned the work of the ministry above the pursuit of intimacy with our God. We had focused on the necessary work of the Kingdom of God above the more crucial cultivation of relationship with God. It's easy to do. Yet it proves so costly.

Still, in His kindness, He wanted to reveal something fundamental. That true ministry is born entirely out of true intimacy. That deep relationship with Him should always be our first focal point. Our first mission. Our first ministry. That all true outward ministry—witnessing, making disciples, singing, preaching, teaching, and serving—always spills effectually as an overflow of a growing, personal relationship with God.

Effective ministry is always and only the fruit of one thing. Active intimacy.

How many ways can we say it? I repeat myself only because I wonder if we truly understand. It's like trying to grasp the wind with a net. We have it. But do we? Help us, Lord. We must understand. Effective ministry is always and only a fruit of one thing. Active intimacy. Fellowship. Friendship. Communion. With God.

THE ROOT AND THE FRUIT

Fruit. I'm often tempted to pass too quickly over that word. What does it mean? Of course, fruit is something birthed out of something else. It is not the starting point. It is the ending point. It is something wonderful and something desired—something we all crave and something we must all produce—spiritual fruit. Yet in order to generate it, we must start by planting seeds. The yield is fantastic. Healthy Kingdom ministry—the fruit—springing up from secret-place time with God—the seed.

Simple. Plant the seed. Produce the fruit.

This was a fairly new idea to me. To us. To Zilch. In fact, I was mostly unaware of it at this point in my life. Even so, it was happening. We were seeing the results. And we were loving it.

Could it be that as we delighted ourselves in Him—first and foremost—that He would flow effortlessly like a river into us, first—refreshing and cleansing us—and then flow wonderfully out of us, impacting the world around us in ways we could never manufacture on our own? We were like little children dancing cheerfully in the center of town, pinching ourselves to make sure it was real.

It couldn't be fake. Right? Honestly, we had grown accustomed—like so many—to the idea that we shouldn't hope for things like revival or transformation or supernatural revelation; so we weren't entirely sure we could trust this moment. That revival stuff was for the grossly naive. Right? We didn't dare step out and believe for something so incredible.

Yet we abandoned reason and dove in. Head first.

We found ourselves cutting songs in the set hoping to descend more quickly upon our potent little worship ditty—the one corporate worship song in our set. Why wait? Come to think of it, why not do more songs like this one? There was something about it. We were drawn to sing any song that would help us—all of us—enjoy God more profoundly. More directly. More fully. More deeply.

The other songs weren't bad. But they were—horizontal. It was different. Somehow. To us. To God. But, of course, *you* understand now much better than *I* did then. Many are raised in this vertical worship culture these days. Or at least near it. (Be careful, though. Just as vertical worship is much more common now, it is also more commonly taken for granted.)

We would often sing "Lord, I Lift Your Name on High" for 20 or 30 or 40 minutes without feeling stuck. Without growing bored or wondering what was next. Why? Because nobody really cared about the song itself. We were truthfully, honestly aiming to lift the name of Jesus on high. We took our time. We lingered in His presence.

Why hurry? We'd even glance occasionally out to the crowd with joy as many were surrendering their hearts to God. Lost in Him. Found in Him. Just as we'd always hoped and prayed they would be. It was something to see. A time to remember.

I think I knew there was more to worship than music, but as I sang that simple chorus with all my heart—often with tears mixed with sweat trickling down my face—an idea began to form. The idea that there was something special about music I had missed. Something special about music that helps us worship. Something special about making a joy-filled noise to the Maker. Unlike any other expression. Unlike any other approach. (But we'll dig into that later in chapter six.)

It was so refreshing. People taking their eyes off of us. Focusing on God. Sure, it was maddening at first—to our flesh—but ultimately it was beautifully freeing. We were no longer required to be rock stars in those moments. We were no longer required to put on a show. We were no longer tethered to the pressure of making something happen. Spiritually.

With the eight songs leading up to that one, we needed to rock people. Move them. Impress them. So much effort went into it. With seemingly little fruit. But then, we were free. Unhindered. We didn't have to electrify anyone with our clothes, our style, or our stage shenanigans. We could simply let go and enjoy God. Together. For real. All the while, enjoying greater fruit as He touched the lives of those worshiping unreservedly alongside us.

Gotee noticed, too. One night, on a little coffeehouse stage in Franklin, Tennessee, president—and friend—Joey Elwood came out to see us. We didn't play often in Nashville. No one did. It was home base. But it was also home of the artistically cynical. That's code for *tough crowd*. Tough as nails.

But Joey wasn't like that.

We played three or four standards from our record and ended with "Lord, I Lift Your Name on High." I remember. He couldn't stop going on afterward about whatever was happening with that final tune. He was blown away. We all were. It was undeniable.

He heard that intangible thing record company presidents listen for—and people of all types, honestly. Something bigger than the band.

It was a memorable night. Still, none of us could put words to what was happening. We only knew we needed more of *that*, whatever *that* was—not so much as a business move, but because it was something we had been searching for. Something beautiful. Something that was stirring things. Shaking things. Breaking things. Something that was bigger than all of us put together. That we didn't control. That we couldn't control. Yet, something we were recklessly drawn to. Even if we didn't understand entirely. We knew God was up to something, and we were compelled to come along for the ride. To discover it. To embrace it.

NO GRID FOR THAT

Things were starting to shift for us. Unbelievably, in the summer of 1998, we found ourselves at a Brownsville Revival worship conference in Pensacola, Florida on a whim, and Lindell Cooley had us dancing for four hours straight—gladly and madly—like fools in God's presence.

We weren't in a worship band. We didn't have a worship album. We didn't consider ourselves worship leaders. But we were wrecked. Undone. And happily. Somehow leading a little movement of hungry worshipers. Somehow becoming hungry worshipers. Things could never be the same. *We* could never be the same.

After much thought and prayer, we agreed with our label, cautiously, to record a full-on Zilch worship CD. Something we had never considered. Something we were still very unsure about. I mean, what could worship music do to touch a hurting world? It's what we do in church, right? We dreamt of playing in bars and clubs, not in churches. We planned on playing music that really moved people. Deeply. Not some empty Christian music. Lacking power and substance. And heart. Certainly, not the music we were used to hearing in church.

It was funny, almost. Even with our newfound experience with the power of worship music—with God's presence—we were tentative. Do you blame us? We had no grid for what we were experiencing. Maybe it would go away. Maybe it wasn't real. Maybe it wasn't enduring.

Think about it. There were no worship songs on the radio. There were no touring worship bands. No Hillsong United. No Bethel. No Elevation. No Passion. No Delirious. No Tomlin. No Redman. No Houton. No Crowder. No Jobe.

There were no worship albums from Third Day, Rebecca St. James, Newsboys, or Michael W. Smith.

Seemed risky. Seemed odd. Even seemed a bit presumptuous.

Fear weighed in. We even banded together as a band—before recording said album—and agreed we'd only record one worship album before making a rapid return to our original Zilch positive pop sounds. Funny thing was, we were only at the beginning of our worship plunge. Just scratching the surface of what would prove to be a deeper dive than anyone knew. Without knowing it, we were on a precipitous descent into worship band land, and we were entirely unaware that, for us, it was a one-way trip.

SONGS ARE ROCKETS

Truthfully, we had no idea where to begin. We knew just enough about worship music to be mildly dangerous. We did know, however, that—whether you're a pop band or a worship band—everything in music hinges on an infectious song. Songs were tools. Songs were help agents. They could serve as rockets to propel would-be worshipers into God's presence. Songs weren't the end. They were a beginning. Potentially a doorway. And a means to connection. A facilitator.

So, we got to work. Writing. Searching.

We'd never intentionally written corporate worship songs. *What's the difference between a song written for a concert versus one written for corporate worship?* We wondered. Every artist—whether pop or worship—wants their songs to be sung. To be shouted from the rooftops. To get stuck in people's heads—and hopefully hearts. We hoped there were a few songwriting strategies we could integrate that might serve to draw people into an authentic pursuit of God. Like we'd experienced with "Lord, I Lift Your Name on High."

We also complied some well-known worship songs we liked, working tirelessly to breathe new life into their arrangements. What if we took these staples, already enjoyed in church—even songs we didn't necessarily jive with musically—and poured a little gasoline on them? You know, just to bring the fire? It started ignorantly. We loved many of the lyrics of these songs, yet struggled to connect with their music. Hmm. Why not blend the music we loved with the lyrics we loved? Later, this would prove to be one of our greatest strengths.

Once we gathered the songs, Gotee gave the thumbs up, and we began recording.

I'll never forget the day Joey stopped by the studio for a visit. We were early in the process. We had tracked all the scratch acoustic and scratch vocal tracks as well as the final drum and bass tracks. That's it. So far.

We were particularly pumped about a little tune from Andy Park called "In the Secret." (Incidentally, if I were to give props to someone who never received any credit for seriously inspiring Sonicflood, it would be to our then youth pastor from Cornerstone Church in Nashville, Tennessee, John McKinzie. I was a volunteer youth worker in those days, and John would take these slower worship tunes from the adult service and rock them out for the students. We worshiped to jazzed-up versions of "In the Secret" and "Open the Eyes of My Heart" all the time. Here's to you, John!)

We hit play on this unfinished gem, and before the last note could fade away, Joey took his money clip and threw it across the room. I had never seen anyone do that before, but we gathered it meant he was happy. He was all smiles. And so were we. We could feel God's fingerprints all over this music. All over this moment. And we hadn't even scratched the surface.

BACK TO THE HEART

About halfway through the recording, we realized God was up to more than we'd imagined. Much, much more. Among other things, it was becoming clear that Zilch wasn't a great name for what He was doing. There's power in a name. But not in our name. We also began to wrestle with the typical "rock band" approach to everything. Photo shoots. Art design. Booking. Autographs. Lights and sound. Travel. Even purpose. Without a doubt, our name—which literally meant "nothing"—appeared to be a serious roadblock.

Could we? Should we? Change our name?

I arrived at the studio one breezy morning. I was scheduled to sing the lead vocal for the lesser-known—now modern worship classic—"Heart of Worship" by Matt Redman. The tracks were finished, and I was alone in the dimly lit control room.

I grabbed the crinkled lyric sheet, hit play, and began to rehearse. And began to weep.

I was only somewhat familiar with this song, but you know how you can *think* you know something, until you actually do? That's what happened to me. I thought I knew this song. I imagined it was simply another catchy worship tune to throw on our growing worship bonfire. I was so wrong.

The song hit me like an avalanche! And I began to worship. There in the studio. But not exactly the way you might picture. It was like God pulled back the curtains to my soul that frail morning. I could barely breathe the lyrics. Hardly get a word out. Barely move. Except to drop to my knees.

I seriously wept there in the studio. In heaviness. It came from somewhere deep within me.

> *I'm sorry Lord for the thing I've made it*
> *When it's all about you*
> *It's all about you, Jesus*

What? Wow. Complete horror. Was it true? Had we made worship about us? Had I made worship about me? About music? About my favorite go-to songs? About the goose bumps? About the rush I felt on a stage?

I had no words.

I grieved, and after a while, I repented. For me. For us. For everything.

Don't get me wrong. My core desire to do ministry was never driven by fame or fortune. I wasn't attempting to build an empire with my name at the pinnacle. I was all about ministry and God and people. I really wanted to make a difference for the Kingdom. I really meant it when I prayed, "Your Kingdom come, your will be done." At least I believed I did.

Yet in that moment, it was as if I was experiencing the weight of the Lord's grief for all of us who had been building our own careers—our own kingdoms—in His name. Trying desperately to ascend the ladder of success. To be heard. To be noticed. To be liked. To be followed. To be somebody. All in the name of ministry. All for the sake of influence. All in the name of worship.

The songs, the charts, the radio singles, the jockeying, the concerts, the interviews, the travel, the photo shoots. What did it all mean? Who was it really for? I wasn't sure. Was it right? Was it wrong? Something needed to shift.

THE SOUND OF WORSHIP

We could feel it increasing as we continued recording. God's Spirit. He was touching us. He was yanking on our marionette strings in ways we couldn't possibly put to words. In ways that were uncomfortable. In ways that were exciting. In ways that made us feel alive. Really alive. And scared too.

A new vision was budding. Our hearts were awakening. Awakening to worship. Our identity was changing. And so, we reasoned, our band name was due a serious awakening as well.

We couldn't be Zilch any longer.

We considered a million different names. Name upon name. List upon list. We petitioned all of our friends. We asked strangers on the street. We had a list a mile long. Yet, we were still at a loss. We tossed around a few we liked—like Flood and Super Sonic Soul. But nothing seemed to stick.

And then, just when we were in the final stages of recording—the mastering phase—our engineer heard us talking about the name change and suggested we put two of the names together. "Why not Sonic *and* Flood?" he kidded.

Huh? I don't think so. We didn't like it. The record company didn't like it. Our families didn't like it.

Sonicflood.

He wrote it on the mastering disc anyway.

Then the next day happened.

We met "worship guru" Ray Hughes. Well, we didn't actually meet him. Yet. We came across an insightful preaching video of his from when he preached at the Brownsville Revival entitled "The Sound of Heaven." Oddly enough, our entire band gathered together reservedly to watch this old-school VHS preaching tape sent to us by our keyboardist's mother-in-law.

Our mouths hung open, jaws on the floor, as he talked about Revelation 19:6, which reads, *"Then I heard again what sounded like the shout of a vast crowd or the roar of mighty ocean waves or the crash of loud thunder: 'Praise the Lord! For the Lord our God, the Almighty reigns.'"*

He zeroed in on the sound of mighty ocean waves, the sound of a massive waterfall like Niagara Falls. He talked about the sound of heaven. The sound of worship. The sound of every creature who ever lived joining together to make one gargantuan sound. A worshiping sound—a sound that would shake the foundations of the earth. And darkness. And dead religion. A billion times more formidable than the roar of Niagara. With exploding praise. Uncapped. Unleashed. Unrestrained. (It seems heaven may be loud after all.)

And the pieces started coming together. A flood of sound. A flood of worship. Worship from every tribe. Every nation. Every tongue. Every people. All pouring out to God. All at once. A massive sound. A sound that would echo for all eternity. The sound of God's people. A spiritual sound. A sound of authenticity. A sound of love. A sound of relationship. A sound of true worship. Of pure worship.

And that's when we ran into Louie. Louie Giglio, that is.

CHAPTER 3

MORE THAN MUSIC

"Show me where you spend your time, money and energy and I'll tell you what you worship."
—JOHN WIMBER

WHILE IN THE midst of a massive, three-month, 75-city Newsboys/ Sonicflood/Beanbag tour, Louie Giglio—founder of Passion Conferences and Passion City Church, pastor, author, speaker, songwriter, etc.—dropped by for a visit. On our little tour bus.

It was the Spring of 2000. Just following the craziness of the Y2K computer scare. Our Sonicflood CD had been out for a year, and we were smack dab in the middle of God's favor. A strange but exceptional time.

Meeting for the first time, we shared some wonderful stories of what God was doing in those days and found we were truly of like heart and mind. Like vision. Like passion.

At one point, after worshiping with us, Louie approached me and graciously apologized. "For what?" I asked. Like many, he said he had at first mistaken us for your basic pop worship cover band. Regurgitating other people's worship songs. In it for the money. Going through the motions. An echo rather than a voice.

Totally understandable, considering the way things can work in the music industry.

I'll never forget. He continued with more affirmation. "There's something special about you. It's like the Holy Spirit has wrapped His arms around you affirming you and all that you are doing—and He is truly accomplishing powerful Kingdom warfare through you."

Wow. Incredible.

Later, he invited us to join him as part of their historic Passion OneDay2000 event outside Memphis, Tennessee. Wow! Dream invite.

Since that first hang, I've learned so much from Louie. Just like you. He's had such a profound impact on this country—this world— concerning worship and passion for God. His unique perspective rips us out of our religious slumber to remind us all of what the songs are really about. What worship is all about. I even added his revelatory book, *The Air I Breathe,* as a mandatory textbook in my upper level Worship Leading class at North Central University. So simple, yet so profound.

Worship. We've all heard plenty of different definitions. Lots of good ones and a few great ones. And likely, most of us have officially bought into the new-not-so-new idea that worship is more than music. Much, much more.

But, I was still learning.

Unfortunately, worship is often still regulated to the 21-minute musical exposé that occurs on Sunday mornings just prior to the sermon. At the same time, some see worship as something that simply happens as they listen to their favorite band or go to a concert to see their favorite arena artist perform.

I get it. It's super easy to misunderstand. We have worship leaders, worship songs, and worship nights. Worship radio, worship books, and worship degrees. And it all points to one thing. Music.

We say things like, "I really enjoyed worship this morning." Or, "I'm going to see my favorite worship leader tonight. Wanna come?" Or, "Worship just isn't the same when Jack Smith isn't leading." And, again, it all points to music.

However, as many are discovering, biblical worship is much more than singing. So much more. Paradoxically, worship isn't meant to rely on music for its sole expression, but musical worship is meant to serve as an expression of a life lived in worship unto God. A life lived in all-the-time relationship. All-the-time fellowship. All-the-time friendship. All-the-time worship. To stand as evidence—as proof—that we are truly living as authentic followers of Christ, inside and outside the walls of the church.

CATEGORICAL WORSHIP

This concept of all-the-time worship was an eye-opening revelation for me when I first began discovering it in those early Sonicflood days. Don't get me wrong. I knew there were things that honored God beyond music, but I didn't grasp the breadth and depth of a life lived in continuous worship. Yet. Not surprisingly, I'm still learning about worship every day from the Holy Spirit, even as I pen these words.

I didn't know each breath could—and should—be worship. I didn't know I could worship God in every moment—or that worshiping Him all the time didn't mean I had to be praying or singing 24/7.

Bob Kauflin explains in his book *Worship Matters*, "After thirty years of leading worship, I've realized that worship isn't just an opportunity to use my musical gifts. It's more than a heightened emotional experience or a way to make a living. It's way more than what we do on Sunday morning. Worship is about what we love. What we live for. It's about who we are before God."[1]

So good. So true. It's about *who* we are and *who* He is in us. All the time.

My son's schoolmate recently slighted him for inviting her to church saying, "Roman, there's more to life than God!"

Oh man. So much is revealed in this little statement. It breaks my heart.

Think of it. Not only is she telling my son to *get a life*, she is also doing what the vast majority of "religious" people do—place God in a category.

Isn't this how many of us think of God? Sometimes unintentionally? Yet completely detrimentally.

Maybe it's because we're so busy. Maybe it's because we're so distracted. Maybe it's because we don't want to imagine God truly touching every part of our lives. And so, we push Him neatly into a little corner called "religion." Compartmentalization at its finest.

The Holy Spirit explained it to me this way. It's simple. We can think of God and His involvement in our lives in a couple of different ways. We can fold Him into our lives in the form of a single category—like work or entertainment or family or sports or travel or finances or school or music or love—or we can surrender ourselves to Him as the firm foundation upon which all the other categories securely rest.

Can you see it? I'm a very visual person, so I actually see a picture in my head of a few little vertical labeled boxes sitting neatly side by side, representing every part of my life—my wife, my children, my work, my vacations, my money, my ministry, my friends, etc. Every category is independent, yet they are all touching each other as part of the activities, people, and experiences that make up my life.

This is the extent of many people's vision for their life. Then, if they "find God," they simply throw up another category next to all the others. The "God" or "religion" category. One of the bazillion others wedged somewhere in the middle of it all—if at all—mostly lost or completely overwhelmed by the endless particulars of the other categories of life.

But this is not the layout of a healthy biblical worldview.

In addition to all of the vertical boxes, there should be another massive box. But this one is not sitting upright—vertically—like the others. No, it is much larger, and it is lying on its side—horizontally—underneath all of the other boxes, supporting them, strengthening them, touching every one.

Do you see the difference? Where do you stand with the boxes in your life? I often have to recalibrate to remember.

What my son's friend didn't grasp is that her statement couldn't be more ignorant. There truly isn't more to life than God. In fact, every other category of our lives is wholly dependent on God. Only exists because of God. Because God allows it to.

Our lives only have meaning because of God. Our lives are only enjoyable because God allows them to be enjoyable. He is the source of all things, and the other categories in life only exist because He supports them—even life as a whole.

FREEDOM FROM GOD

"Wait a minute!" you say. "There are many people who have enjoyable and meaningful lives apart from God."

Seemingly so.

But have we considered this? Just because many deny God's existence doesn't mean He removes His touch from their lives. No. If He did, it would mean certain death. For no one can exist apart from God. Maybe that's what we all want in our flesh. To be left alone. For God to back off and let us live our lives. But unbeknownst to many, this is impossible. For all things are held together by God through Christ (see Col. 1:17). The truth? If God decided to completely release people from His care, from His power, from His presence—as many say they desire—it would mean far more disastrous repercussions than we realize.

Isn't this what it means to be out of God's presence? Maybe this is exactly what hell will be like. After doing everything He can to woo us to His side—to love and care for us—when it all comes down to it, God will finally give some folks exactly what they desire. Life without Him. Life without His presence. But it won't be what they imagined. Finally. Rid of God. Rid of His incessant nagging. His outrageous and primeval rules. Yes. Finally. On my own. To do whatever it is I desire. Free from God.

But life apart from God isn't possible. Because life without God's presence is hell.

There is no breathing without God. There is no thinking without God. There is no standing without God. There is no working without God. If He pulls out, we simply fall to the ground in a heap of flesh and bone.

Life apart from God isn't possible. Because life without God's presence is hell.

If He detaches Himself from a person—or even, say, a nation—that person, that nation, is lost.

If God embodies everything that is good, then to be apart from God—separated from His presence, His life, His face, His power, His grace—is to be separated from everything that is good and pure and right. It is to be in the worst conceivable place.

Hell.

Therefore, as much as we may endeavor to do so, it is impossible to relegate God to a compartment alongside all the other compartments of our lives. He touches every category of our lives whether we accept it, desire it, approve of it, or not.

Why is this so important to a biblical understanding of worship? Well, because it is impossible for relationship with God to be regulated to our musical worship. To our songs. To our church services. To a single hour during a single day of the week.

Of course, we can attempt to ignore Him during the other times in our lives, but He is continually calling us to place Him on the throne of each area. Each category. He is calling us to worship Him in our work, in our relationships, in our family, in our sexuality, in our finances, in our words, in our thoughts, in our entrepreneurship, in our eating, in our delights, and in our sadness.

Why? Because worship is life. And life is worship.

WORSHIP IS LIFE

Giglio's definition of worship from his book *The Air I Breathe* continues to clarify things: "Worship is our response, both personal and corporate, to God—for who He is! and what He has done! expressed in and by the things we say and the way we live."[2]

Sure, musical worship is found in there somewhere. I suppose it falls into the category of "the things we say," along with the things we preach or pray. And the rest, of course—which is the vast majority—refers to the "way we live." It encompasses everything else in our lives—our work, our entertainment, our relationships, our thoughts, our joys, our pains—especially those things that reach beyond the lyrics streaming from our mouths during a church service or in our secret times with God. Though it includes these things as well.

Poignantly, the way we handle our business dealings and our finances certainly exhibits our heart for worship as much as how we sing in church. Probably more.

Think of Ananias and Sapphira in Acts 5. We see it as no big thing to lift our praises to God on Sunday and then cheat Him and others a little on Monday. Think again. The fact is, *the songs our lives sing in the marketplace are much louder than the songs our mouths sing in the church place.*

Ananias and Sapphira were carried out of the house stone-cold dead. Why? Not because they weren't a part of the worshiping church community, but because they lied to the Holy Spirit in their business dealings. (And yes, though dramatic in nature, this is New Testament, post-resurrection theology—code for "it happened after Jesus died and was raised from the dead.") Even so, we are tempted to brush our hand across our forehead in relief, mistaking God's silence in our lives for His approval, even while death of a different kind—spiritual rather than physical—quietly but cunningly pursues us.

It's the same in every other area of our lives.

Even as my heart was awakening toward musical worship, I was also understanding the bigger picture. How we speak to our spouse, our parents, and our kids reveals our love for God even more than our church attendance. How we lend a hand to others in need is certainly just as worshipful—or worshipless—as lifting a hand in the sanctuary. How we spend our Friday nights is likely more revelatory of our heart for God than how we spend our Sunday mornings. Though all of it is important.

Yes, it was all beginning to make sense to me, even as we were rounding out that undying Newsboys tour. Worship is life. Every breath. Every word. Every thought. Every deed. In public. In private. Everything. Everywhere. Which is kind of scary, I realized.

Truthfully, I was much more comfortable with classifying things as either God stuff or personal stuff. Church stuff or family stuff. Spiritual stuff or work stuff. Worship stuff or non-worship stuff. But the truth is, all of our stuff is God's stuff, and all of the stuff He gives us is stuff that was meant to bring Him glory. And if we aren't bringing glory to God with our stuff—because we are compartmentalizing our stuff or abusing His stuff—we must renew our perspective that we might worship Him with all of our moments, with all of our stuff, in every category of our lives.

NOTES

1. Bob Kauflin, *Worship Matters* (Wheaton, IL: Crossway Books, 2008), 17.
2. Louie Giglio, *The Air I Breathe* (Colorado Springs: Multnomah, 2017), 43.

CHAPTER 4

IN THE MAJESTIC AND THE MUNDANE

"God wants worshipers before workers;
indeed, the only acceptable workers are those
who have learned the lost art of worship."
—A. W. TOZER

IT'S IRONIC. SOME of us are more inclined to process worship in terms of music, while others become annoyed when music—in any sense—is considered in the conversation. I understand. To a point. As mentioned in the previous chapter, there is now a fairly clear understanding within the global Church that everything in our lives—big or small—can and should be an expression of worship toward God. Everything. Including music.

While music is not the end-all, be-all of worship, neither should it be excluded from the conversation for posterity's sake. If the entirety of our lives is meant to be an act of worship, and music is a part of our lives, then music must also be included as potential worship. We shouldn't throw the baby out with the bathwater. For the baby is not the issue. The bathwater is.

Of course, singing isn't inherently worship. But neither is anything else. Including attending church, giving to the poor, or sharing the Gospel. All of these things *can* be done with a heart of worship toward God—or not. Singing was created to bring glory to God, but it can also glorify other things, like self or even the kingdom of darkness. It all depends on the motivation behind it—behind any action, truthfully.

Even so, when it finally sinks in that sliding up under a beat-up old pickup and using our two hands to restore it to its former glory can be just as worshipful as lifting those two hands during a song, our perspective is finally awakening to God's vision for worship. For our lives.

How about flying a plane? Worship. Especially in a storm! (Incidentally, I wonder if pilots purposely loosen up on the controls sometimes, all with the intention of helping us worship with a little more fervency as we zip like a bullet through the choppy night skies.)

How about teaching math? Landscaping? Writing computer code? Cleaning toilets? Doing homework? Coaching? Real Estate? Writing a book? Yep. All worship. When we do these things by faith and for the purpose and glory of the Lord, they certainly serve as worship to God. Because anything that honors or exalts the Lord is worship to Him. Including loving your spouse, showering compassion on your children, or helping your neighbor snow-blow her driveway. (Yes, I live in Minnesota.)

News flash. Just because we don't do our work unto God doesn't mean it ceases to be worship. It just ceases to be worship to God.

As discussed, we tend to compartmentalize our lives. But this new "worship is life" approach helps us realize that just as spending time with God in the secret place—reading the Word, praying, and singing to Him—is worship, so are the seemingly not-so-spiritual details of our lives. The potential is all there. We just need to realize it. Be aware of it. Walk in it.

Richard Foster implores us; "Cause every task of your day to be a sacred ministry to the Lord. However mundane your duties, for you they are a sacrament."

Whether it's the routine task of taking out the trash or the celebrated opportunity to do something grand on the world's stage, we are meant to worship God in the majestic and the mundane.

STEERING CLEAR OF DO-DO

As with most things, there must be balance. The same is true for understanding our work as worship.

After finding myself out of the band, Sonicflood, in May 2000, I began to have a little bit of a crisis of "doing." Like many, I was wrestling with my identity, realizing that I had been allowing my Kingdom "doing"—my ministry—to define my identity more than my Kingdom "becoming."

I came across Revelation 2:2,4. Here, Jesus remarked, *"I know all the things you do. ...But I have this complaint against you. You don't love me or each other as you did at first!"*

As adults, what's the first thing we ask someone when we're meeting them for the first time? "So uh, what do you do?" Why? Because in our modern culture, we mostly identify ourselves and others by what we do. Yet, as you may have guessed, this is not God's design. In fact, He refuses to allow us to live for long in a world where we are defined firstly by what we do. He is more interested in who we are than in what we do. Unfortunately, we've come too far to turn back so easily, right?

What's the first thing we ask a teenager about his or her future? "What do you want to do when you grow up?" Truth is, we often say, "What do you want to *be* when you grow up?" But when we say *be*, we actually mean *do*. Yes?

Here's the point.

We are so incredibly consumed with *doing* that we often miss our purpose altogether. As a result, we absolutely risk losing our *being* all while trying to prove our worth through *doing*.

Over and over, young people came to me—especially in those Sonicflood days—asking, "What do I need to do to do what you do?"

And I would purposefully frustrate them a little by answering, "You just need to seek first the Kingdom of God and His righteousness, and then everything else will take care of itself."

"No, yeah. Absolutely," they'd respond. "But seriously, what should I do if I want to do what you do?"

And then I would repeat with a smile, "Matthew 6:33. Seek first the Kingdom of God." We'd laugh, then discuss the idea further, and I'd give them a little practical advice as well.

Haven't you noticed, though? This drive? To do, to accomplish, to succeed? It's becoming more and more overbearing with each passing day—as each generation looks to make their mark on the world. To feel significant. To be noticed. To be discovered.

It's not that God doesn't want these things for us. For us to do great things for Him. To overcome. To stand strong. To help the helpless. To reach the lost. To give to the poor. To accomplish impossible tasks. To worship *through* our doing.

This is all wonderful!

The problem is, we go about it backwards.

BECOMING PRECEDES DOING

In our passion for doing great things for the Kingdom, we often put the cart before the horse. (Whatever that means.) We become so busy chasing accomplishment that we overlook the source—the One from whom all good deeds originate.

Isn't it God who plans good deeds for us to do? *"For we are God's masterpiece. He has created us anew in Christ Jesus, so that we can do the good things he planned for us long ago"* (Eph. 2:10).

We've seen others do great things, and we're taught to do them as well—dream big dreams, set monumental goals—because "nothing is impossible with God," right? And this is largely accurate. Yet we fall prey to common errors. We believe we will *become* someone great because we *do* something great, when this is exactly the opposite of the truth. Exactly opposite of how Kingdom greatness occurs.

Don't get me wrong. Good deeds play a huge part in God's plan for our lives. James 2:26 reminds us, *"Just as the body is dead without breath, so also faith is dead without good works."* Here we see that good works done in faith actually prove we are alive in Christ. We even read about scores of people in the Bible who accomplished remarkable deeds, and this inspires us, helping us remember their worshipful contribution to the Kingdom.

> We believe we will become someone great because we do something great, when this is exactly the opposite of the truth.

Yet God's plan has never been for us to achieve greatness as a result of doing great things, but to do great things as a result of the greatness He has put within us.

Another way to say it?

Our greatness in Christ is not born out of the great things we have done. The great things we have done are born out of our greatness in Christ.

It's often said, "We are not human *doings*. We are human *beings*." The point? We are not defined by what we do as much as by who we are. And who we are—our character—is much more valuable to God than what we do.

Even so, let's back this train up a little further.

If *being*, not *doing*, marks our greatness in Christ, where does *being* originate?

SEEK FIRST

In Hosea 6:3,6, Hosea declares:

> *Oh that we might know the Lord! Let us press on to know him. He will respond to us as surely as the arrival of dawn or the coming of rains in early spring...I want you to show*

love; not offer sacrifices. I want you to know me more than I want burnt offerings."

Paul reminds us in Philippians 3:8, *"Yes, everything else is worthless when compared with the infinite value of knowing Christ Jesus my Lord."*

Interestingly, it is this issue of knowing—or not knowing—God that Jesus brings up again in Matthew 7, concerning those He welcomes into His Kingdom. He declares, *"On judgment day many will say to me, 'Lord! Lord! We prophesied in your name and cast out demons in your name and performed many miracles in your name.' But I will reply, 'I never knew you. Get away from me'"* (Matt. 7:22-23).

Intense.

> **Knowing God leads to being godly, which leads to doing great things for God.**

What we uncover in these verses is that knowing God always precedes being godly, and being godly always precedes doing Kingdom good deeds. Or better said, *knowing* God leads to *being* godly, which leads to *doing* great things for God.

Not the other way around.

Okay. Got it.

But how then do we *know* God?

Easy, right?

Easy, but not easy. Because we make it difficult.

> *But seek first his kingdom and his righteousness, and all these things will be given to you as well* (Matthew 6:33 NIV).

Clearly this verse is primarily there to remind us to stop worrying about things like food and clothing. But it also suggests an order to things. Jesus is saying, "Trust me. I've got you. You don't have to worry about the basic things. Like food and shelter. Like making a way for yourselves. Seek me first. Everything in your life flows best out of our relationship."

*"If you **look** for me wholeheartedly, you will find me. I will be found by you," says the Lord* (Jeremiah 29:13-14).

Do you want to do great things for God? Do you want to make a difference for the Kingdom? So do I. Do you want to leave your mark on this world by serving and helping and giving and loving? In music, dance, theater, or writing? As an accountant, lawyer, physician, or in IT?

Seek first. God. Your God. Your friend. Your Father.

Then you won't find yourself worrying about your *doing* at the expense of your *being*.

More than anything, God has designed us to walk and talk with Him. To be one with Him. To fellowship with Him. To *be* together.

Clearly, He has plans for us to *do* great things together with Him as well. But, graciously, He won't allow us to make this our chief aim. Our chief aim is to know Him. Our *doing* together flows beautifully out of our *being* together. When we seek Him first, heavenly deeds will always follow. But when we pursue *doing* as our priority, we labor in vain. By ourselves. Without His help and without His blessing. And without fellowship. Then we find ourselves alone, striving to do, do, do, do. And, we end up wallowing all alone in do-do. (Pun intended).

Doing is the fruit of a life lived in God. *Seeking* Him is the seed that must be planted in order to bear the fruit of good deeds.

Plant the seed. Water. Cultivate. And the fruit of good deeds will grow. Out of the soil of healthy relationship.

Seek God first, and you will truly begin to know Him. *Know* Him, and you will truly begin to become like Him. *Become* more like your Father in heaven, and out will flow—like a crystal-clean stream—wonderful, beautiful, God-designed, God-sanctioned,

God-empowered works that bring glory to the King and touch the earth.

We must cease *doing* with hopes of *becoming*. It's impossible anyway. Instead, we begin with *seeking*, which turns into *knowing*, which turns into *becoming*, which produces Kingdom *doing*. Which in turn becomes worship unto God. Yes. This is the progression by which our work becomes worship. It happens when our work is born out of intimate relationship with our heavenly Father. All by faith. All for His glory. All in His power.

A.W. Tozer says it as good as anyone; "No one can long worship God in spirit and in truth before the obligation to holy service becomes too strong to resist. Fellowship with God leads straight to obedience and good works. That is the divine order and it can never be reversed."

Even so, I didn't have a clue what God's presence was in those days. And I've come to realize there is even more confusion on this topic than I realized.

CHAPTER 5

GOD'S PRESENCE— WHAT IS IT?

*"If we must 'feel' God's presence before
we believe he is with us, we again reduce
God to our ability to grasp him."*
—CRAIG S. KEENER

WE HEAR A lot of folks say or sing things like, "We want more of your presence," or "There's just nothing like His presence." But what exactly is the presence of God? Does it come? Can it leave? Is it an "it" or what? I didn't know exactly. And I supposed, if I was going to be a leader of musical worship, I should have some idea.

One night, while leading worship at a large conference, I heard the Holy Spirit tell me to remind everyone of this lesser-known fact— that we can spend time singing worship songs, reading the Bible, and going to church, and yet still never actually encounter God's presence. *What? Wait.* I was learning in this moment too.

Do you mean to tell me that God's presence isn't solely found in the soft music we often encounter during an altar call near the end of a service?

What? Could it be true? And, moreover, if the source of God's presence isn't music, what is it?

I was talking with my two oldest boys recently, and what I heard myself say—inspired by the Holy Spirit—helped me better understand. I wanted them to realize that simply reading the Bible each morning wouldn't guarantee they had actually spent time in God's presence.

I asked my son, Roman, "Is it possible to treat reading the Bible like you might a job?" Like an assignment to be accomplished? Like an item on a to-do list? Couldn't we read a chapter here and a chapter there, and then close the Good Book never having specifically encountered God in relationship?

Isn't that what happened to many of the Bible's religious leaders? The Pharisees and Sadducees certainly read the Word and knew the Word, but somehow, in the process, they didn't manage to connect with the God of the Word.

My son's eyes lit up. "Yeah, sometimes I just read the words and don't actually think about what I'm reading. I can even read a whole chapter without thinking about or interacting with God at all."

Now we're getting somewhere.

CLOCKING IN AND OUT

Is it possible that many of us churchgoers approach spiritual disciplines this way too? Oh, I don't think we mean to, but we could be missing the point. The idea is not to check off an item on a to-do list or clock in to accomplish the spiritual onus for the day. The idea is to engage with God Himself. As strange as it may sound, reading the Bible, praying, and singing are not at all what we're after anyway.

Truth be told. We don't read the Word of God so we can know the Word of God, but so we can know the God of the Word. In the same way, we don't sing songs to God to remind Him of how awesome He is. We sing songs to remind ourselves of this. Likewise, prayer is not a means of acquiring the "what" that we want from God, but of acquiring the "who" that we need in God.

Being *with* God, having fellowship *with* Him—this is our primary aspiration. Spiritual disciplines are simply a means to that end, a vehicle to aid in rocketing us into richer fellowship with our Creator.

Imagine. I'm sitting in the same room as my wife. It certainly could be said that we are in each other's presence, yes? But isn't it also possible that while we may physically be in the same room, we may also be completely disconnected—one daydreaming while the other consumes a good book? If so, are we actually in each other's presence? Physically, yes, but relationally, no.

> *We don't read the Word of God so we can know the Word of God, but so we can know the God of the Word.*

Incidentally, this may contribute to modern-day marital problems more than we realize. We might say, "I don't know what happened. We went on dates every Friday night, but the relationship still dried up." Not surprisingly, being in a restaurant together on our phones and then sitting side by side in a theater does not constitute being *with* our spouse. Just because we find ourselves in the same room, communicating via text and Facebook or living in the same house—in each other's physical presence—does not mean we are joined relationally.

Scary as this may sound, couldn't it also be true that we might find ourselves physically present with other believers, in nice buildings with atmospheric sights and sounds, singing God-drenched songs, listening to poignant preaching, and still be completely unengaged—intentionally or unintentionally—with the Maker Himself? Still *not* in His presence?

Is this possible? Is this happening? I believe so. More than we care to imagine.

Granted, God's presence is somewhat of a mysterious thing—something that can be difficult to wrap our minds around—but I'm hoping we can demystify it a bit. In fact, I'd like to suggest that His presence is not as enigmatic as it might seem.

Maybe being in God's presence is much the same as being in a friend's presence after all. When I am directly engaged with my friend, I am truly in his presence. When I am not directly engaged with my friend, the relationship is not growing as much as it could be, even if we are physically in the same space.

"But God's presence is all around us, right? Isn't He, uh...oh, what's that term...ever-present? Um, omnipresent?"

Yes, He is Emmanuel—God, always with us. So quite possibly, the question we really need to be asking is not so much if God is present with us but whether we are present with Him. Maybe we don't need to worry so much about whether God will show up in our lives or in our services, but rather, if we will show up in His presence. Will we be present in His presence?

Read that again.

Ephesians 3:12 states, *"Because of Christ and our faith in him, we can now come boldly and confidently into God's presence."* And Hebrews 4:16 invites, *"So let us come boldly to the throne of our gracious God. There we will receive his mercy, and we will find grace to help us when we need it most."*

Come boldly.

This is His clear and biblical invitation to us. To step boldly into His presence. Not to beg Him to step into ours. To engage boldly in relationship with Him. Not to sit on the sidelines hoping and praying that He will make Himself available to us. But to respond boldly to His available presence by running straight into His arms. Not because of what we've done, but because of who He is.

NOT IN THE MUSIC

By accepting God's invitation to come boldly into His presence, we are not saying that God's presence is incapable of coming or going. Sure. His presence does, as we say, "manifest."

Biblically, there are two types of God's presence. His omnipresence—that is, in essence, God always everywhere. And His manifest presence—that is, His person, His glory. Tangibly filling a room in a way that can be sensed or felt or experienced, and possibly even seen.

Wow. If you grew up like me, you may have to sit down for that one.

Yet, as I mentioned, God's presence isn't found in the music.

Wait for it.

How often do we make a direct connection between God's tangible presence and the music we enjoy in our worship services? This is a good thing. Mostly. Yet if we're not careful, we can all but limit God's ability to touch our lives to the 17 minutes of music we experience on Sunday morning. Or to those warm, fuzzy keyboard tones floating somewhere underneath the pastor's hyper-anointed words during an altar response or near the end of a service.

Ah, yes. There it is. God's presence is here. The keyboard is emanating perfectly.

I remember we used to jokingly refer to that keyboard patch as the "Holy Spirit." Sorry. Funny, not funny.

I agree. Something does seem to shift as the keyboardist begins to tickle the ivories. We've all heard it. Everything is going along just so, and then, all of a sudden, the piano starts playing. And suddenly, this triggers a different quality of voice from the pastor. The atmosphere seems to change. Crazy, right?

But we must not forget—music is only a tool. It can certainly aid us as we endeavor to come boldly into God's presence, but the keyboard, the music—in and of itself—is not His presence.

It might seem trite to say it that way, but this is exactly what I sensed God was asking us to process. And I needed to understand it for myself. To make sure I wasn't simply connecting with a comforting sound but with the Comforter. To be positive that I wasn't simply enjoying peaceful melodies but that I was encountering the Prince of Peace.

Ultimately, music itself should not be what we're seeking—the end-all, be-all. No. Our eyes should not be set on music, but on the One who created music.

Big difference.

NOT IN A BUILDING

Just as God's presence isn't found in the music, it doesn't reside exclusively within a church building—as if He longingly waves goodbye when we depart for Sunday brunch, eagerly awaiting our return to His "house" next week so we might once again enjoy sweet fellowship together.

No. God's presence is always available, accessible. God Himself is always available, accessible. Everywhere. Inside and outside of the church building. It is we who leave. It is we who remove ourselves from His presence, from Him. It is we who clock in. And clock out.

This was new for me. Again, what if we didn't need to spend as much time pleading for God to show up in our services after all? What if the real issue was simply, will *we* show up? Will *we* be present in His presence?

God's presence isn't something out there. Something intangible. Something I hope to lure into my song service. If I sing loud enough or dance wildly enough. It is *Him*. His person. It is not a glory cloud or a fierce emotion or even an "it." *He* is "It." And it is Him I seek. God Himself. My God. My King. My Friend.

This is one of the reasons I quickly determined to remain cautious when I sing songs like the Grammy award-winning "Holy Spirit." I love it, and I've led it a million times. And people gravitate toward it something fierce. Even so, sometimes I pause to clarify a little right before singing it.

Holy Spirit, you are welcome here
Come flood this place and fill the atmosphere
Your glory, God, is what our hearts long for
To be overcome by your presence, Lord

These lyrics are powerful. Potent. And I'm not suggesting there is anything inherently incorrect here. However, there is a risk of misunderstanding that can occur when we sing them unaware.

First, when we ask the Spirit to *flood this place and fill the atmosphere*, we are speaking to the manifest presence of God. The element of His presence that can come and go, that can move. This is not bad. But it can tend to thrust us unknowingly in a direction that is more in line with old covenant thinking. This idea is more likely to get us seeking after a God who fills a room. A God who gives us goose bumps. A God who comes when we sing the songs just right, but who leaves when we don't. A God who is only around when the worship music and the preaching is anointed and "next level." A God who is most powerful, most prevalent, most present in a church service or in a church building.

This can cause our pendulum to swing too far to one side.

Acts 7:48 reads, *"However, the Most High doesn't live in temples made by human hands."*

It's not that God doesn't or can't fill up a room. It's just that emphasizing this part of His presence can more easily extinguish the New Testament, new-covenant revelation of God alive in us. In His people. In each one of us. It can easily frustrate the foundational New Testament living-temple theology.

Amazingly, even Solomon himself—who lived long before Peter wrote about the living stones and the living temple in First Peter 2:5—indicated he understood this idea when he penned First Kings 8:27 after constructing the first true physical temple of God: *"But will God really live on earth? Why, even the highest heavens cannot contain you. How much less this Temple I have built!"*

First Corinthians 3:16 explains, *"Don't you realize that all of you together are the temple of God and that the Spirit of God lives in you?"*

Ephesians 2:21-22 adds, *"We are carefully joined together in him, becoming a holy temple for the Lord. Through him you Gentiles are also being made part of this dwelling where God lives by his Spirit."*

This dwelling where God lives? A spiritual temple of sorts. Made up of His people. Living stones. Built into one. The place of God's abiding.

I wondered if it was simply a matter of semantics. But it became clearer and clearer with each verse I uncovered. These were truly and deeply foundational principles established by the apostles as part of a God-breathed way of life.

NOT AN IT

As with any worship lyric, when we sing something like, *"Your glory, God, is what our hearts long for,"* we need to stop and ask ourselves if this is really accurate. Is God's glory the essence of what we long for? More than anything else?

This is a reasonable question. If it is true, we quickly move on. If it is not. We adjust.

I would like to contend that God's glory is truly not what our hearts desire. In fact, His glory is not at all what we are seeking. Not at all what will fill our souls. Not at all what will satisfy.

Forgive me if I am oversimplifying here, but God's glory is not Him. It is that which surrounds Him. It's the part that explodes out of who He is. The part we see and try to explain. His radiance. His sparkle. His glow. His power. His majesty. His authority.

You might say, "But you can't separate God from His glory."

Maybe.

Yet, I can't help but picture the scene in Daniel 10 where Daniel has a vision of Christ and attempts to explain "the flashes like lightning" coming from His face. John the beloved recounts a similar vision in Revelation 1, describing Jesus' face to be "as bright as the sun in all its brilliance." Luminous. Explosive. Glorious. Magnificent.

These are all incredible things that attempt to describe Him. That surround Him. Yet they are not Him.

Is it the lightning flashes that radiate from His face that we seek? Is it His radiance or His sparkle? It is the sword coming out of His mouth? It seems obvious. No. It is not His bronze shimmering feet or His voice that thunders like mighty ocean waves or His eyes that shine like flames of fire that we desire. It is God Himself that we seek. It is not God's beauty that we long for. It is God Himself. It is not God's power or strength or wonder or honor or splendor that we crave. It is His person. The person of God is what we long for. It is *who* we require.

God does embody all of these great things, but there is a trap hidden here. In fact, I began to uncover the subtle ploy of the enemy to get us to view God as an "it." To think of His presence as an inanimate object. As a some*thing* rather than a some*one*. As a *what* instead of a *who*.

As you might guess, 99 times out of 100 we will be less successful engaging with a something than a someone. We can be sure, engaging with God as a someone—and not as a something—is the aim.

Think of it. We can't engage relationally with feet that shimmer as bronze. We can't walk and talk with power or brilliance. We can't even fellowship with glory! We can only abide in, live in, commune meaningfully with the person of God. Not His traits. Not even His character. But with Him. In Him.

Truly, when we say we have encountered God's presence, we are suggesting we have come face to face with Him, His person, His being—not simply His traits. And certainly, not simply a feeling or an emotion or a pleasant song.

Sure, there are often incredible feelings and emotions present when we encounter His presence, but most of these feelings can also be experienced apart from His presence. So it cannot be our feelings that prove His presence but our relationship.

Be careful! Too many folks encounter God's true presence and then mistakenly tie it to the emotions they experienced in the moment they encountered Him. Then, in an attempt to recreate the experience, they seek the emotions rather than seeking the person of God. And they then miss Him altogether.

Stop. Reread. Process. Tremble.

Psalm 106:20 reminds us that Israel exchanged their glorious God for the statue of a grass-eating ox. If we truly want Him—and I am sure we do—we must end our pursuit—even our worship—of beautiful music, gifted leaders, and emotionally charged ambiance. We must recognize our tendency to wrongly identify an encounter with artists and atmospheres as an encounter with God.

We must recognize our tendency to wrongly identify an encounter with artists and atmospheres as an encounter with God.

If we truly desire Him—His presence—we must waken from the stupor of mistaking God's presence for the rush we feel during a powerful service, or even the exhilaration we experience that comes from enjoying others connecting with God. He is so much more than this. When all is said and done, we must find ourselves engaged with the person of God, pursuing poignant relationship with Him, fully present in His presence.

CHAPTER 6

AIDING OUR AWAKENING WITH SINGING

"The gift of language combined with the gift of song was given to man that he should proclaim the Word of God through music."
—MARTIN LUTHER

NOW THAT WE'VE gone entirely out of our way to establish that music is not the sole contributor in worship, let's circle back and discuss the significance of musical worship, especially as it pertains to singing. Yes, as diligent as we must be in continuing to clarify the obvious—that worship cannot be confined to a few fleeting musical moments before a sermon—*we must also come to grips with the fact that worshiping God through singing itself is something uniquely powerful and entirely biblical that cannot be ignored.*

You can be sure I am uniquely determined to keep from overemphasizing musical worship. At the same time let's not underemphasize it either. The Bible clearly emphasizes it—even highlights it—and in doing so establishes its notable significance in aiding our awakening toward an ever-increasing, intimate relationship with God.

Paul Baloche stated in his book *God Songs*, "Worship is not music, but music can be worship."[1]

Think of it. There are two vastly different types of sound that can come out of your mouth. With a split-second flip of the larynx, you can go from speaking to singing. Whether this seems like a big deal to you or not, it's certainly worth pondering.

Why did God make us capable of creating these two types of sounds? Speaking and singing, both flowing out of the same mouth, off the same tongue, through the same lips. Yet with sounds that are so extraordinarily different? We understand that speaking is foundational to the human existence. But what about singing? Is it less important? Is it more important? Is it the same? Certainly, singing is something the vast majority of the seven billion people on the planet can do. In some way, shape, or form. Should it then be an afterthought?

SOMETHING ABOUT A SONG

Songs touch our lives as few things do. The moment a song from our past begins to play, it's as if we are transported instantaneously to the spot we first heard it. Your first concert. Those roller rink days. Your senior prom. Ah yes. I'll never forget my first prom. "In the Air Tonight" from Phil Collins. So good. So smooth. Greatest drum fill of all time.

Songs serve as marker points for our lives. Good and bad. Songs inspire us. Motivate us. Infuriate us. Songs get our tired toes tapping. Our weary hands clapping. Our hardened hearts hoping. And our furrowed lips humming.

Probably one of the greatest compliments I've ever received was when a young lady came up to me after a night of worship and said these words: "Thank you for your songs, Jeff. They help me say all the things to God I've wanted to say but didn't know how to."

David clearly understood the power of a song. For self-expression, primarily. For better or for worse, he used these singable sonnets like a bull in a china shop at times, blasting everyone in his path. Enemies. God. Circumstances. Evil. Everything. Then, on a dime, he'd turn and transform into the mesmerizing psalm-whisperer he's so famous for.

It's no secret. The Bible is filled to the brim with singing Scriptures, many of which are surprisingly found outside the Psalms. Scriptures that tie the cultivation of a deeper, more joyful walk with God directly to singing.

> *There the Israelites sang this song: "Spring up, O well! Yes, sing its praises!"* (Numbers 21:17)
>
> *Listen, you kings! Pay attention, you mighty rulers! For I will sing to the Lord. I will make music to the Lord, the God of Israel* (Judges 5:3).
>
> *I will be filled with joy because of you. I will sing praises to your name, O Most High* (Psalm 9:2).
>
> *That I might sing praises to you and not be silent. O Lord my God, I will give you thanks forever!* (Psalm 30:12)
>
> *Sing to the Lord, for he has done wonderful things. Make known his praise around the world* (Isaiah 12:5).
>
> *Sing to the Lord! Praise the Lord! For though I was poor and needy, he rescued me from my oppressors* (Jeremiah 20:13).
>
> *Sing, O daughter of Zion; shout aloud, O Israel! Be glad and rejoice with all your heart, O daughter of Jerusalem!* (Zephaniah 3:14)

We could certainly highlight a hundred verses like these throughout the Old Testament and still not come to the end of them. Their sheer number exhibits the weight the Bible places on worship through singing. Even so—and surprising to some—there are many similar verses sprinkled throughout the New Testament as well.

> *Well then, what shall I do? I will pray in the spirit, and I will also pray in words I understand. I will sing in the*

spirit, and I will also sing in words I understand (1 Corinthians 14:15).

Well, my brothers and sisters, let's summarize. When you meet together, one will sing, another will teach, another will tell some special revelation God has given, one will speak in tongues, and another will interpret what is said. But everything that is done must strengthen all of you (1 Corinthians 14:26).

Don't be drunk with wine, because that will ruin your life. Instead, be filled with the Holy Spirit, singing psalms and hymns and spiritual songs among yourselves, and making music to the Lord in your hearts (Ephesians 5:18-19).

Are any of you suffering hardships? You should pray. Are any of you happy? You should sing praises (James 5:13).

SOMETHING ABOUT SINGING

We understand that singing itself cannot render for us an authentic, relational connection with God. But biblical truth does suggest that people who are actively involved in cultivating an authentic relationship with God will be found singing.

Why?

Singing is a command.

God's commands are not burdensome but designed to be wonderfully life-giving. Truthfully, we short-circuit our own lives when we cease to follow His ways. Singing to God benefits us, and we must mature beyond the point of walking in offense when He *requires* something of us that is good.

Singing is a tool to help us make deeper connections with truth.

Think the ABC song or the songs kids sing to help remember the days of the week or the 50 states. It stands to reason, then, that our theology can become much more deeply rooted in our hearts when we not only hear it preached and see it in print but when we sing it as well.

Singing helps strengthen our faith.

Ironically, it is not God who needs to hear my praises. He certainly appreciates them and engages relationally, but it is *my ears* that need to hear *my mouth* sing the praises of God. These praises flow out of my mouth, into my ears, and back down into my heart again, rooting my faith upon the rock-solid foundation of God's Word.

Singing destroys the enemy.

When confronted with the attacking armies of the Moabites and Ammonites, Jehoshaphat boldly sought the Lord. God responded through Jahaziel with one of the most quoted battle passages of all time: *"Do not be afraid! Don't be discouraged by this mighty army, for the battle is not yours, but God's"* (2 Chron. 20:15).

Singing is something unique that can be done corporately, birthing a single expression of praise from a multitude of worshipers.

After gathering the Israelites to humble themselves before the Lord in worship and thanksgiving, Jehoshaphat famously led his army out to war, setting the singers at the front. In verse 22, the Bible describes, *"At the very moment they began to sing and give praise, the Lord caused the armies of Ammon, Moab, and Mount Seir to start fighting among themselves."* Incredibly, it was as the people sang these words: "Give thanks to the Lord; his faithful love endures forever!" that God fought and won the battle for His people. He does the same for us today.

Singing builds community.

As a worship leader, I have traveled extensively. Occasionally, I've enjoyed being a part of an experiment where the organizers scattered different stations around the room focused on repentance, communion, journaling, drawing, poetry, etc. All with a desire to add depth to our worship expressions beyond singing. I love it!

Even so, it occurred to me that *worship in song nicely facilitates something that none of these other forms of worship can. Togetherness.* Think about it. Can we all journal together, creating a single expression of love to God with a group of 100 or more? No. Journaling is very useful, but it is best done autonomously. The same goes for poetry, drawing, and repentance. But not singing. Singing is something unique that can be done corporately with all of God's people, thereby birthing a single expression of praise from a multitude of worshipers.

Singing is modeled by God himself.

It's true. Zephaniah 3:17 helps to affirm the age-old truth that God never asks us to do anything He Himself hasn't done already. Not surprisingly, singing is no exception.

> *For the Lord your God is living among you. He is a mighty savior. He will take delight in you with gladness. With his love, he will calm all your fears. He will rejoice over you with joyful songs.*

We could preach a whole series on this one verse—and I will attempt to drive this point home later in Chapter 10—but suffice it to say we did not initiate this thing called singing. We did not choose to love Him. He chose to love us. Worship through song is simply our fitting and crucial response to all that God has already done in pouring out His great and wonderful love toward us.

WHEN SONGS BECOME PRAYERS

As I traveled the world leading musical worship in the early 2000s, the Lord started showing me the incredible connection between songs and prayers—so much so that I actually began thinking of worship songs as prayers set to music. It may have been obvious to some, but I didn't notice the clear similarities. Truly, worship songs and prayers share many of the same components and serve many of the same purposes.

Understanding this helps us as leaders, writers, and congregants as we seek to become more intentional in both expressions.

Prayers serve as a powerful expression for believers. From the intercession of Daniel, to the repentance of David, to the appeal for favor from Esther, to the desperate cry for help from Jehoshaphat, prayer takes on many forms. From Israel's plea for deliverance, to Jesus' prayers of thanksgiving, to Moses's face-to-face fellowship with God, prayer is a foundational connect-point for God's people and their Creator.

So, what about worship in song? Is it much different?

We tend to define worship music simply as songs sung with the purpose of bringing glory to God—either via songs sung *to* God or *about* God. This is clearly a significant part of musical worship, but couldn't there be more?

As you know, I didn't grow up in a church where we equated the singing portion of the service with actual time spent cultivating relationship with God. Yet as my eyes were opened to this idea years later, I found myself gravitating passionately toward songs with lyrics that were sung straight to my Father in heaven. Honestly, I loved these savory, new songs-to-God so much that I almost avoided songs-about-God entirely. Only in the last few years have I swung the pendulum back toward the center where I now seek out and lead all types of worship songs. Songs to God. Songs about God. Songs that proclaim. Songs that rally. Songs that prophesy. Songs that convict. Songs that inspire.

Just as different prayer emphases have numerous facets, worship lyrics do as well. In fact, the longer I travel this winding road, the greater my understanding of musical worship becomes—and the greater my realization of the connection between prayer and musical worship.

Since early Bible times, prayer and musical worship have been attached at the hip. The psalms are loaded with musical prayers, and it is often remarkably difficult to tell where the psalmists' prayers end and their songs begin.

I love how James Goll writes it in his book *The Lost Art of Pure Worship*: "Worship and prayer form the seamless garment the priest wears as he ministers unto the Lord. Where does worship end and prayer begin? In my experience, they just ebb and flow together like the tides of the ocean, supernaturally-naturally. In the ministry of the priesthood of all believers, I see no clear demarcation between something called 'worship' and something called 'prayer.'"[2]

Even in Revelation 5:8-10, we find the prayers and the songs of God's people intertwined.

> *And when he took the scroll, the four living beings and the twenty-four elders fell down before the Lamb. **Each one had a harp, and they held gold bowls filled with incense, which are the prayers of God's people.** And they sang a new song with these words: "You are worthy to take the scroll and break its seals and open it. For you were slaughtered, and your blood has ransomed people for God from every tribe and language and people and nation. And you have caused them to become a Kingdom of priests for our God. And they will reign on the earth."*

Verse 8 refers to something many call "harp and bowl," where the music brought before the throne (the harp) is intermixed with the prayers of God's people (incense in a bowl) until it is all brought forth in a powerful, worshipful expression—a new song!

What if we were to take our favorite song lyrics and simply pray them—speak them to God? Would it work? What if we were to take our private prayers and layer in melodies? Could this be effective?

Take the recent song, "Even So Come," from Passion—a song that aligns itself with Revelation 22:17-20 by hastening Jesus' second coming with the simple word, "Come."

"Even So Come"

All of creation
All of the earth
Make straight a highway
A path for the Lord

Jesus is coming soon
Call back the sinner
Wake up the saint
Let every nation shout of Your fame
Jesus is coming soon
Like a bride waiting for her groom
We'll be a Church ready for You
Every heart longing for our King
We sing, "Even so come, Lord Jesus, come

There's also the song of intercession I wrote back in 2001. It's a perfect example of a song that seeks to agree with what God desires, praying it out through singing—in order that these things, which are the established will of God, might come to pass!

"Let Me Burn"

Let the nations rejoice in you
Let your people return to you
Let the source of my life be you
Let me burn for you.
Let your fire of justice reign
Let creation confess your name
Turn my heart from stone to clay
Let me burn with praise

Now, flip it around, and consider these common prayer acrostics we often follow.

P — Praise	**A** — Adoration
R — Repent	**C** — Confession
A — Ask	**T** — Thanksgiving
Y — Yield	**S** — Supplication

Aren't these prayer themes entirely compatible with those in our worship songs? Repentance and confession might be the least familiar, but maybe this serves as a wake-up call for more songs with these types of lyrics.

Don't get me wrong. I'm not suggesting prayer and singing are entirely one and the same. Yet if there is a reason to see them as close cousins, it is that just as prayer is clearly meant to procure direct communion with the Holy One, these songs of worship are meant to provide for us complete, unhindered, laser-like, straight-to-the-throne access to God as well.

We know this. But it is easy to forget—to get caught up in other things.

Worship through song is simply our fitting and crucial response to all that God has already done in pouring out His great and wonderful love toward us.

Because our worship music has adopted such powerful expressions involving well-known bands, concert-like atmospheres, and songs we sing in our cars and services alike, we must be careful not to miss the Father in all the hoopla. He, above all else, desires relationship. He, above all else, knows we need relationship. He, above all else, calls us to intimacy, fellowship, and communion with Himself—through prayers, through songs, and in our everyday lives.

Once again, I've discovered that my ears desperately need to hear my own prayers. Compellingly, I've even heard God's voice as I or others pray. I've learned from these prayers—sung or spoken. Likewise, my ears need to hear my mouth singing biblical truths from the Word again and again—whether they come through reading the Bible or via those little ditties we call "worship songs" (which could certainly be referred to as "responsive readings set to music").

Consequently, just as this worship leader's heart needs to come into direct contact with God through prayers—musical or otherwise—so do those who are being led. And so, I must become more intentional as a worship leader, checking the lyrics as I choose my songs. And as I set out to write the worship songs of tomorrow.

Yes. If songs are simply sung prayers and prayers engage us with God, then our songs should be intentional in connecting us directly to God in the same way that prayer brings us directly before His throne. For when songs become prayers and prayers become songs, we might just find ourselves stepping into deeper dimensions of His presence than we've ever imagined.

NOTES

1.   Paul Baloche, Jimmy Owens, and Carol Owens, *God Songs* (Lindale, TX: Leadworship.com, 2004), 23.

2.   Jim W. Goll, *The Lost Art of Pure Worship* (Shippensburg, PA: Destiny Image Pub., 2012), 95.

SECTION 2

WHY WORSHIP, ANYWAY?

CHAPTER 7

WORSHIP IS NOT FOR GOD

*"The Christian does not go to the temple to worship.
The Christian takes the temple with him or her."*
—RAVI ZACHARIAS

HAVE YOU EVER heard someone—in the context of musical worship—shout out something like, "It's all about you, Jesus"?

I absolutely adore this assertion. Why? Because it reveals a sincere heart. A heart that desires to keep the pure focus of worship off one's self and directly on our heavenly Father. A heart that burns—like John the Baptist—to decrease so that our Lord and Savior might increase.

Beautiful.

That said, let's take a fresh look at why we worship and who it's all for, anyway.

First, I want to present a familiar idea from a flipped perspective—one that, I believe, has often been misunderstood. Here it is:

Worship is not *for* God. It is *about* God and *to* God, but it is *for* you and me.

What a difference a preposition can make.

Unbeknownst to me, upon hearing this statement tumble out of my mouth, I encountered several folks who assumed immediately that I was quoting Victoria Olsteen. Ha! And I thought it was a Deyo original!

She did utter something similar, but alas, I am not quoting Mrs. Olsteen. Nor am I trying to say what she said, which was exactly this: "Do good because God wants you to be happy. When you come to church, when you worship Him, you're not doing it for God, really. You're doing it for yourself, because that's what makes God happy. Amen?"

Truthfully, I'm not entirely sure what she was saying. Exactly. Though I do have a hunch.

Of course, I imagine the word *happy* is a word that may turn some folks off when considering spiritual things. Some folks, including me. I have a feeling, however, that if she had reworded her statement a tad, we might have ended up very near the same page. Her statement, "When you worship Him, you're not doing it for God," is similar to what I said on the previous page. But before you roll your eyes—please continue on.

Clearly, our worship is always to be aimed at, focused toward, and passionately given to our one and only true Creator God. He is the singular object of our worship. He is the solitary reason we worship. He is the only being truly worthy of worship. He is God. And there is no substitute. Period.

But this is not the issue at hand.

The issue—and I believe it is an important one—is the overall purpose of worship. It's function. What is the point? What is the *reason* we worship God?

No doubt, the chief end of worship is to glorify God. And I don't disagree. At all.

But the question underlying is, why does a massive, eternal, infinite, uncreated God who is perfect and holy and entirely self-contained want me—an imperfect, created, finite piece of dust—to worship Him? How does my worship help Him receive anything

He doesn't already have? How does my worship actually bring Him glory? Can it, does it, could it add anything to Him at all?

You see, if we resolve—as many do—that the chief end of worship is to bring God glory, we may in return begin to wonder what type of God could need or want glory from us. From there, we may be compelled to ask, if indeed God does receive glory from us through worship—*how* exactly does He receive this so-called glory?

Good question. Glad you asked.

WIRED FOR WORSHIP

Maybe it's not so much that He receives glory directly from our worship. Maybe He receives glory—which Victoria imprecisely referred to as "happiness"—not so much as a result of our songs of praise but as a result of us doing exactly what we were *made* to do—which is, of course, to worship Him.

Pause. Reread. Process.

Following, it would stand to reason that when God's creation does what He designed it to do, He receives honor and glory—which, I suppose, could or would make Him...er, uh, well..."happy." It seems this could also make anyone who loves God—angels, humans, and all created things—"happy."

Undoubtedly.

Why? Because when we are doing what we were made to do, we are not doing what we were not made to do, and when we are not doing what we were not made to do, that is a wonderful, glory-giving response! For when we are doing what we were made to do, it stands to reason that we are in better standing with God than otherwise, which clearly opens the door for Him to open the windows of heaven and pour out true Kingdom blessings upon His creation—which, of course, would make anyone and everyone in their right mind...happy!

Whew. Breathe.

Many of those who take issue with Victoria's statement do so because they don't like the idea of someone saying, "If we worship God, it will make Him happy, and then, in return, He will bless us. And then we will be happy, and rich, and beautiful, and problem-free, and successful, and have a fancy car, and live in a perfect house, and nothing in all the world will ever, ever, ever go wrong. Ever again. Just like the Olsteens. Fist bump."

And, of course, they would be right in taking issue with this type of rationale. But I'm sure Victoria would agree. This type of theology just doesn't make sense when considering the many teachings of Jesus, His own excruciating pain and suffering, and the great list of others in the New Testament who endured such treacherous times. I don't envision the word "happiness" being used very regularly in these settings.

For me, when I make my statement—that worship is *about* God and *to* God, but *for* us—I am *not* referring to our happiness. I am endeavoring to answer the unrelenting question, "Why does God want us to worship Him?"

Consider this statement from God Himself.

> *I have no complaint about your sacrifices or the burnt offerings you constantly offer. But I do not need the bulls from your barns or the goats from your pens. For all the animals of the forest are mine, and I own the cattle on a thousand hills. I know every bird on the mountains, and all the animals of the field are mine. If I were hungry, I would not tell you, for all the world is mine and everything in it. Do I eat the meat of bulls? Do I drink the blood of goats?* (Psalm 50:8-13)

This is one of my absolute favorite passages, because it gives us deep insight into who God is—the person of God—and into what His ultimate purpose is for worship. It pulls back the curtain—if only for a moment—that we might catch a tiny glimpse of what truly makes Him tick.

Interestingly, God answers some questions here that no one is actually asking. Out loud. But we can be sure they were rolling around like bowling balls inside everyone's head.

Questions like: "Why do we have to keep bringing these animal sacrifices to God, anyway?" And, "Why does He give us animals to enjoy and then turn around and ask for them back?" You can even hear people from enemy nations poking fun, saying, "If your God is so marvelous, why are you constantly required to bring Him supper?"

This sounds ridiculous, but when enough people start asking offensive questions about God, we tend to get a little embarrassed.

Even so, God answers these questions and, in doing so, clarifies the obvious.

He says, "Look. This sacrifice thing. It's not for me. It's for you. I'm not asking you to bring me animals because I need them, but because *you* need to bring them. I don't need the blood of goats or the meat of rams. I'm not hungry. Or thirsty. And even if I were, I definitely wouldn't come to you to fulfill my needs. Don't you see? I'm doing this for you! I'm requiring you to bring me worship because *you* need it, not because I need it. I am self-sufficient. Perfect in all my ways. I have no needs. None. Zilch. Nada. It's all mine. The animals. The wood. The fire. I made them all. They belong to me alone. Why would I *need* you to bring these sacrifices to me? I don't *need* anything, and I certainly don't *need* you to worship me. I do enjoy relationship with you. But most of all, I wired you to *need* to worship me. When you worship me, it does not fulfill a need I have, but it fulfills a foundational need you have. Do you understand?"

WORSHIP BENEFITS

Paul pays tribute to Psalm 50 when he writes in Acts 17:24-25, *"He is the God who made the world and everything in it. Since he is Lord of heaven and earth, he doesn't live in man-made temples, and human hands can't serve his needs—for he has no needs. He himself gives life and breath to everything, and he satisfies every need."*

Wow.

Imagine. I buy a shiny, brand-new Ford Explorer. I take it to the gas station for its first official fill-up. I notice the sticker that reads *unleaded gasoline only*. I fill 'er up and then drive home. Once home, I decide to write a friendly note to the Ford Company. It reads:

> Dear Henry, I wanted you to know that I filled up my new Ford Explorer with unleaded gasoline today, just as you instructed. I knew you'd be so happy when you found out! Hope you have a great day! Sincerely, Jeff Deyo

First off. The folks at the Ford Company's initial reaction would certainly be to pass my letter around the office for a good laugh. Clearly, the directive to only put unleaded gasoline in my car was not given primarily for the benefit of the maker, but for the driver.

As hinted, I'm sure the Ford Company received a little "glory" when they realized an owner of one of their cars followed their instructions, but the ultimate benefits of following the car maker's instructions go to the driver, not the maker. Which leads us to another important question.

Even though God does not need us, He does want us.

Who benefits from worship the most? God or man?

If it is true that God has no needs and that His worth cannot be increased or decreased by our worship, then it stands to reason that the overall benefit of worshiping God is less His than it is ours.

Of course, I'm not saying God receives nothing from our worship. He surely does. In a sense, He receives the one thing He desires. Relationship with us.

However, the distinction is that God does not need relationship with us. This may shock you, but God does not need us. And truthfully, this is great news. Who would want to worship an infinite God who needed His finite creation? The best news? Even though God does not need us, He does want us. And He cherishes relationship with us.

Quite honestly, with this knowledge, we should be bouncing off the walls with joy! Why? Because, serving a God who *wants* our worship is way more attractive than serving a God who *needs* it.

A DIFFERENT KIND OF BLESSING

For us, there is a torrent of blessings attached to worshiping God. Not always blessings in the way we define them—money, cars, new shoes, happiness, and sunny days—but blessings in the way God defines them—truer peace, sweeter sleep, richer relationships, greater hope, and a wonderfully secure eternity.

Of course, God does not promise that all our days will be sunny. Days without struggle. Days without pain. Days without trials. In fact, He actually promises that hardships will continually be a part of the believer's journey. At the same time, He promises to be with us, giving us the power to overcome. Giving us the power to walk *through* the valley of the shadow of death. Not always over or around it. He vows that our spiritual muscles will be exercised—and vigorously built up—when we face these promised persecutions. In fact, this is one of His greatest strategies for strengthening the muscles of our faith.

Even so, it can certainly be said that when we live according to God's directions—including His command to worship—there are great blessings for us in this life and the next. Things like unstopped ears as we listen closely to His voice. Diminished pride as we shout, bow, and lift our hands. Greater freedom as we dance and celebrate our deliverance from sin and death. Stronger community as we inspire each other to love and walk closer with God.

The blessings of worship keep on giving and giving. And these blessings from worship—from God—are clearly meant for us. Clearly.

In fact, this principle is true not only for worship but for every other gift from God. Each one is *about* God but *for* us. Think of it. Is salvation *for* God? No. It is *about* Him, but it is *for* us! Is forgiveness *for* God? No. It is *about* Him, but it is *for* us! Is healing *for* God? No, it is *about* Him and *from* Him, but it is *for* us! Is the gift of the Holy Spirit *for* God? No, it is completely *about* Him, but it is *for* us!

I love to say it this way. The benefits of worship are ours. God wired us to *need* to worship Him. He knows that our hearts desperately need to hear our mouths declare the incredible truths about Him. Of course, He already knows these truths. It's not Him who needs to be reminded. It's us!

Check out my man, Isaiah. Chapter 40, verse 16 blows our minds by reminding us of this incredible truth—that all the forests of the world do not contain sufficient fuel to make a sacrifice large enough to rightly honor our God.

Big God alert.

In the same way, there are simply not enough songs or voices—even if every mouth of every person who ever lived sang every worship song that was ever written throughout all of human history, all at the same time—to bring God all the glory He so richly deserves. We could sing 24 hours a day, seven days a week, 365 days a year for ten billion lifetimes, and still our worship would stand insufficient.

Like a drop in the bucket.

Remember. *It's my ears that need to hear my mouth declare the perfections of God. Not His.* It's me who is changed as I lift my hands or bow my knees to my Creator. Not Him. It's my own heart that is set free when I dance before Him or sing in harmony with His people. Not His. It's my perspective than is renewed when I stand trembling before Him in awe and wonder. Not His.

Truth is, once we get past the obvious—that God alone is to be worshiped, and that all worship must be directed to Him and only Him—we quickly realize that worship is not really about God at all—it's all about us. It's true! He made us to worship, and He made worship for us!

CHAPTER 8

THE MOST IMPORTANT ONE THING

"Do you want to be near him in the age to come? Demonstrate it by living close now."

—Bob Sorge

FOR AS LONG as I can remember, I have enjoyed watching the Denver Broncos play football, whether they're winning Super Bowl L (50) or losing it all. I grew up in the Rocky Mountain state during my elementary school years, and my parents still live there today, so Denver is like a second home for our family.

Strange to some, I even enjoy listening to the press interviews with the Broncos' coaches during the off-season. Mostly because I love learning about how they approach leadership. I find it fascinating how they motivate their players to work so passionately toward achieving one thing—a common goal. I learn about focus and dedication. About never giving up and leaving it all on the field. About teamwork and, of course, self-discipline.

I am especially intrigued by how they convince all of these highly gifted, high-profile athletes to play so unselfishly when it comes to the role they've been assigned. Quarterback. Left guard. Nose tackle.

Gunner. Wide receiver. Each man focused on one task. One role. One goal. One thing. For the good of the whole team.

In the NFL, we all know what that one thing is. Winning the Super Bowl, of course. But how does one team make this happen? Especially when so many teams are fighting for the same prize? Here's the most common theme I hear: "Do…your…job." Yep, they preach it over and over again. If each individual player will simply play the role he has been assigned with great passion, focus, and attention to detail, the whole team will overcome. Together.

This type of thinking primes me to ask some questions when it comes to Christianity. When it comes to life.

What is the most important thing to do in life? What is the one thing we can all rally around? Why are we here? What is our purpose? As we breathe air in and out of our lungs on this big round rock hurtling across the universe, what exactly is it we should be doing after all? Are we simply here to take up space in the atmosphere, or is there something more? Seriously. Out of everything we could put our energies toward over a lifetime—all of the bazillion options—what is it that really matters? Where should we start? Where should we end?

LIVING WITH THE END IN MIND

Some people call it living with the end in mind. This is a life-altering concept. Ponder it. How do you want to feel the moment you leave this earth? When we arrive on that fateful day, when we breathe in our final fragile breath—just before we exhale—what will be going through our mind? Will we be satisfied? Will we have questions? Will we have regrets? What, if anything, will we wish we had done differently?

Somehow, I imagine we will have a remarkably different perspective right in that moment. Everything will come flooding into view, as if we are using our eyes for the very first time.

A few months before my mom's mother passed away, I had the chance to ask her, "If you could do anything different with your life, what would you do?" Without blinking, she quickly said, "I would have read my Bible more." Interesting. Out of everything she could have put on her "do over" list, this is what she said? We weren't having a conversation about spiritual things. I was simply hoping to learn something from someone who had experienced more in life than I. With hopes that she—because she was likely nearer to her end than I—could help me see things more clearly. In order to live with my end in mind.

Ecclesiastes 7:2-4 instructs, *"Better to spend your time at funerals than at parties. After all, everyone dies—so the living should take this to heart. Sorrow is better than laughter, for sadness has a refining influence on us. A wise person thinks a lot about death, while a fool thinks only about having a good time."*

Wild.

This is not to suggest that we should be consumed with death, but that we should be sober concerning the stark reality of our life's end—not that we would shrink back from it, but that we would boldly prepare for it.

On that fateful day, when we finally come face to face with God, it is unlikely we will wish we'd spent more time building our business—away from family. It is unlikely we will wish we'd taken more spectacular vacations or spent more time on our social media platforms. No. Undoubtedly, we will feel overwhelmingly like my grandmother did. We will wish we had spent more time in the Word and *with* the Word. *With* Jesus. Like Mary.

AT THE FEET OF JESUS

If we had the courage to honestly ask the ten-million-dollar question—what is the most important thing in life—I am convinced we would all come away with the same conclusion. Evangelism? Discipleship? Dreaming big? Serving the widow and the orphan? Obedience? Loving others?

No.

If you've been paying attention, you know, of course, where I'm going. And of course, you realize we're starting with the assumption that our answer must originate from the Scriptures. So, here it is: *to walk and talk with God in a deep and personal relationship for all of eternity—just as Adam and Eve did.* All else exists only to serve this one single ambition.

One lady understood. And Jesus recognized her for it in Luke 10.

> *As Jesus and the disciples continued on their way to Jerusalem, they came to a certain village where a woman named Martha welcomed him into her home. Her sister, Mary, sat at the Lord's feet, listening to what he taught. But Martha was distracted by the big dinner she was preparing. She came to Jesus and said, "Lord, doesn't it seem unfair to you that my sister just sits here while I do all the work? Tell her to come and help me." But the Lord said to her, "My dear Martha, you are worried and upset over all these details! There is only one thing worth being concerned about. Mary has discovered it, and it will not be taken away from her"* (Luke 10:38-42).

Clearly, Jesus is emphasizing something important here with the idea that we should learn from Mary. He highlights the fact that when given a choice between working the to-do list and sitting at the feet of the Master, the priority must be sitting at the feet of the Master.

By no means is Jesus condemning work, as we've already discussed. He is helping us prioritize. Paul reminds us in Second Thessalonians 3:10 that those who refuse to work should not eat. Clearly, work is not a bad thing in itself. On the contrary, work can and should be very spiritual. Very worshipful. Work—and the enjoyment in it—is part of God's gift to man. But work—like anything else—becomes empty and fruitless when it exists as a priority over relationship with God. Over communion and fellowship with God.

Jesus is sounding an alarm. Do you hear it blaring? When we are consumed with work—or anything—more so than being consumed with God, things will always be out of balance. That's just the way He made it. Why? To safeguard us from attempting to look to anything besides fellowship with Him for fulfillment in life. And to keep us from sinking into many other lies like fear, worry, apathy, and stress.

Maybe the issue with Martha wasn't so much that she was consumed with work but that she was consumed with worry. Did you notice what Jesus said to her? He mentioned her worry in connection with all that needed to be done for the party. And He reminded her that there is truly only one thing worth being concerned about.

> Our work is not the root of our relationship with God. It is the fruit.

And if we're going to be concerned, it might as well be something worth being concerned about. Our relationship with God.

Some may contend that their work is the primary means by which they commune with God. But this is not His principal design. As mentioned in Chapter 4, *our work is not the root of our relationship with God. It is the fruit.* In fact, our best work—truly Kingdom work—only produces healthy fruit when we first plant the seeds of fellowship with God. Relationship spawns good deeds. Friendship yields good works. Communion produces good fruit. *Work is fully spiritual when—and only when—it grows out of pure and genuine relationship with the One who created both man and work.*

Did you notice? The passage above also points out that Martha was distracted. Ever been there? Martha literally had the Savior of the world right there in her house, eating her food, sitting on her couch, enjoying her home; yet she was so consumed by other things that she couldn't even stop to take it all in. To appreciate the moment. To enjoy her Savior. Not even for a moment.

Why? Because of fear.

I mean, what would happen if she stopped working? What would happen if the food didn't get prepared? What would happen if everyone forgot about the feast that was planned, and they all just sat feasting at the Savior's feet instead?

The world wouldn't *stop* spinning. In fact, quite possibly, some folks' worlds might *start* spinning. For the very first time! Martha's reputation would not be ruined. No one would fault her for this fortunate misfortune. Why? Because the One who holds all things together was standing before them. Right there. In their midst.

What else could matter?

Yet we scurry around as if the fate of the earth is hanging in the balance and we're the only ones who can keep the scales from tipping. All the while, Jesus is calling us to settle down. To stop all the rattled rushing. To come and enjoy Him. To sink into fellowship with Him.

My friend and fellow worship leader, Elisha St. James, put it like this on Instagram recently: "It appears in this day and age that more people are interested in ministry than they are in God."

Ouch.

TWO THINGS

Jesus was crystal clear regarding His primary passions for us. When asked in Matthew 22:36, *"Teacher, which is the most important commandment in the law of Moses?"* He replied, quoting Deuteronomy 6:5 and Leviticus 19:18, saying, *"'You must love the Lord your God with all your heart, all your soul, and all your mind.' This is the first and greatest commandment. A second is equally important: 'Love your neighbor as yourself.' The entire law and all the demands of the prophets are based on these two commandments"* (Matt. 22:37-40).

The entire law? You mean all of the dos and don'ts generously scattered throughout the Bible can be summed up with these two commands?

Why didn't you say so?

When I first recognized this, it brought me more relief than I can adequately communicate. Like you, I can often become overwhelmed by all that the Bible demands—all that is required of us as believers in a day and age when so little attention is given to God's "antiquated" commandments.

With this revelation, however, I was reinvigorated. If I struggled in my little day-in-and-day-out life to keep it all straight—and I knew I did—all I had to remember was, "Love God. Love people."

Even I could jive with that!

In fact, after Martha and I started having children, we made this phrase our family motto. Love God. Love people. Yes sir. We figured this would help us communicate the complexities of the Gospel in a way that children—and Pharisees—can better understand.

For years now, each morning before our kids walk out the door to school, I holler, "Two things?" And they holler back, "Love God. Love people."

Conveniently, we, as a family, process everything we do through these two imperatives—which, in reality, are one single imperative. You see, when we love and worship God, we become more like Him. And when we become more like Him, we start loving what He loves. And, of course, He loves people. So, these two imperatives fuse mystifyingly into one. One. Beautiful. Thing.

As expected, the Good Book is chock-full of passages that aim fiercely to point our heading in this one simple direction. Toward one main thing.

FIRST LOVE

Jesus boldly raises the issue of "one thing" with the church at Ephesus in Revelation 2:2-5:

> *I know all the things you do. I have seen your hard work and your patient endurance. I know you don't tolerate evil people. You have examined the claims of those who say they are apostles but are not. You have discovered they are liars. You have patiently suffered for me without quitting. But I have this complaint against you. You don't love me or each*

other as you did at first! Look how far you have fallen!
Turn back to me and do the works you did at first. If you
don't repent, I will come and remove your lampstand from
its place among the churches.

Look closely at the emphasis. Like many of us, the Ephesian church had placed great prominence on *doing*. On work. On ministry. Too great. Why? Because it's very easy to do.

Yet Jesus rebuked them sternly for it—even though they were truly doing "good" work. Clearly it was no minor dilemma in His mind. He exclaimed, "Look how far you've fallen!" From what? From love. Loving Jesus and loving others.

The Greek translation for verse 4 literally reads, "You have lost your first love."

Lost is a strong word.

It's not as though they had simply lost their footing or stumbled a wee bit. No. They had plummeted over the cliff. To the point where they actually valued ministry, doctrine, and righteous living more than intimacy with God. Ha! Poor fools. But wait. This happens to many a well-meaning Christian leader every day, and thrice on Sunday. To you! To us! It was a grievous enough concern that Jesus demanded repentance while firmly warning them of their impending removal from among the churches.

Think that's crazy?

THE GREAT COMMANDMENT

Jesus is even more exacting in Matthew 7:21-23 when He rebukes those who prophesy, cast out demons, and perform miracles in His name without having relationship with Him. What? Yes.

We looked at these verses earlier, but they deserve a closer look.

What does He say? What is His emphasis?

You didn't work hard enough? You didn't raise enough money? You didn't put enough energy into helping the poor or serving the widow? No. He says, *"But I will reply, 'I never knew you. Get away from me, you who break God's laws.'"*

At first glance, it appears He is focusing primarily on disobedience. But look closely. His disappointment is ultimately tied to relationship. How so? Because obedience is all about relationship. Obedience is the fruit of relationship. It's how we know the tree is healthy. It's how we know relationship exists in the first place.

Jesus affirmed this in John 14:15: *"If you love me, obey my commandments."* You see, obedience is not some special ticket granting us admission into relationship with God. This would grant us salvation through works. No. Obedience is simply the proof that we actually have relationship with God.

The telltale phrase in Matthew 7:23 is, *"I never knew you."*

This passage can mess with your mind a little bit. Or a lot a bit. Seriously. Is it really possible to perform miracles or cast out demons without walking in real relationship with God? Woah. Hold on.

Breathe.

Before we explode our brains trudging over this theological land mine, let's look at the obvious. Once again, Jesus breaks it down— hoping we will come to grips with where to concentrate our greatest efforts. Yes, ministry is *wonderful*. Beyond a shadow of a doubt. We can easily quote a thousand verses that spur us on to good deeds.

Go and make disciples. Preach the Gospel. Serve the poor. Help the widow. Heal the sick. It's all in there. Yet, as author David Ferguson reminds us in his book *The Great Commandment Principle*, "In desiring to accomplish the Great Commission we must never overlook the Great Commandment."[2] For it is in fulfilling the Great Commandment—to love God and to love people—that we are afforded the wherewithal to fulfill the Great Commission.

ONE WITH CHRIST

Paul doesn't avoid this topic. In fact, as mentioned in Chapter 4, his writings are some of the most famous on the subject.

I once thought these things were valuable, but now I consider them worthless because of what Christ has done. Yes, everything else is worthless when compared with the infinite value of knowing Christ Jesus my Lord. For his sake I have discarded everything else, counting it all as garbage, so that I could gain Christ and become one with him (Philippians 3:7-9).

The King James Version uses the word *dung* instead of garbage, and while that certainly sounds more revolting, I just can't get a certain picture out of my head. You know. That time I casually strolled through the garage and was viciously punched in the gut by a hideous, rotting stench. You've smelled it. The one where multitudes of maggots are wriggling up and down, all throughout the bottom of your receptacle like warm little contaminated grains of rice. So nasty! Almost like they're crawling all over your body right now.

Ever had to clean that thing?

Paul is doing his best to convey the gravity of the situation. Think of it. He actually suggests that compared to knowing Christ, everything else—service, good deeds, offerings, evangelism, church attendance, service to the poor, everything—is as repulsive to God as those little maggots are to us. Basically, ministry *for* God apart from intimacy *with* God is like the rotting stench of the worst garbage dump, outhouse, or barnyard you've ever known.

But we're not finished yet.

Jesus again weighs in aggressively in John 17:21 when He prays to His Father concerning you and me. What does He pray? That we would do ministry like He did? No. That we would sell our possessions and give the money to the poor? No. That we would share the Gospel to the uttermost parts of the earth? No.

He prays this one thing—that we would be one with the Father, just as Jesus is one with the Father. In fellowship. In friendship. And why? So that the world would believe.

Of course, He's not—I'm not—saying these other things are unimportant. They are truly vital! It's just that Jesus is frantically attempting to clarify what we miss so effortlessly—that everything we want to accomplish in life and in ministry will ever only be accomplished as it flows out of one thing. True relationship with the Father.

Did you catch it in His prayer above? The aftermath of God's people becoming one with Jesus and the Father is effective evangelism. "So that the world would believe." Transformative ministry. The fruit of true intimacy.

Heide Baker invites us to embrace this truth; "It is out of this place of intimate worship that the fragrance of his love and glory flows to the world around me. Lasting fruit comes from no other place."[3]

Viable, authorized ministry from the heaven can and will only occur as a result of abundant communion with the Father, Son, and Holy Spirit. God will not allow it to exist long term in any other form. This is not the bad news. It is the best news. Why? Because God understands our overwhelming tendency to attempt to fraudulently bolster our identity through ministry—at the expense of intimacy. And He will not allow this—because He loves us and because He knows there is no higher goal than togetherness with Him in relationship. Everything else is born out of this one thing.

David jumps aboard the one-thing train in Psalm 27:4 echoing a beautiful theme: *"The one thing I ask of the Lord—the thing I seek most—is to live in the house of the Lord all the days of my life, delighting in the Lord's perfections and meditating in his Temple."*

David's one thing is framed differently, but it is still the same one thing. Relationship with God. When he says he wants to live in the house of the Lord all the days of his life, he is not referring to his desire to hang out in a church building or to remain safely inside his little Israelite-only bubble. No. The house of the Lord represents a place—a spiritual place—where all of us come together as a community in fellowship—the place where we all live and have our being, together in God. With God. Forever.

If there is anything to desire. If there is anything to chase after. If there is anything to covet. If we must lose all we have to gain one thing—this is that one thing. Intimacy. With the Father of all Creation. Yes, God Himself is the treasure in the middle of the field. He is the prize that makes selling everything else we have worth it.

One goal.

One passion.

One thing.

THE JESUS NUT

Ever heard of a Jesus freak? How about a Jesus nut?

Many helicopters, like the UH-1 Iroquois, have a single large nut—the main-rotor-retaining nut—that holds the main rotor to the mast. Interestingly, this particular nut has been nicknamed "the Jesus nut" by its awesome aerial operators. Why? Well, because "the Jesus nut" is the single piece of hardware that holds the propeller to the body of the helicopter—which means, if that nut fails, you can kiss yourself goodbye. It's over. You are going down, and there is no force on earth that will change that fact. The Jesus nut represents a single point of failure that—if broken—will bring forth catastrophic consequences.

> Salvation is not the one thing. It is the thing that makes the one thing possible.

We should imagine our relationship with Jesus similarly. Not salvation, but relationship. You see, this may come as a shock, but salvation is not what we're after either. Salvation is simply a means to an end. Salvation is the thing that makes relationship with Jesus, with God, possible. Salvation is not the one thing. It is the thing that makes the one thing possible. And while we should be filled with rejoicing over our salvation, we must understand that salvation itself is not the point. Relationship with God—this one thing—is ultimately what matters.

If our relationship with God is weakened and then severed or broken, then everything else in our lives is ultimately going to fail. It's as if our souls are the helicopter—the vehicle that transports ministry and good works to others, while relationship with God is the nut that holds it all together. If the relationship nut fails—if we get sidetracked and forget to keep our heart set on our first love—than our lives will inevitably come crashing down into a world of hurt, demolished by the tremendous weight of ministry.

GOD'S WISH LIST

I don't want to continue pounding away at this, but I simply cannot stress the importance of cultivating intimacy with God enough. I am much too aware of my own temptations to put the work of the ministry ahead of my relationship with God. Even the writing of this book! Plus, if you haven't noticed, the Bible is overrun with teaching after teaching on the topic.

I wonder why?

Maybe because it's a serious issue. Maybe because God recognizes our need to reprioritize our time with Him and is desperately attempting to help us return the one thing back to the top of our list.

Speaking of lists. Did you know God has a wish list? Just like us? Yet the beautiful thing about God's wish list is that He—unlike us—always gets what He wishes for.

I discovered His wish list when I ran across Isaiah 11:6-9.

> *In that day the wolf and the lamb will live together; the leopard will lie down with the baby goat. The calf and the yearling will be safe with the lion, and a little child will lead them all. The cow will graze near the bear. The cub and the calf will lie down together. The lion will eat hay*

like a cow. The baby will play safely near the hole of a cobra. Yes, a little child will put its hand in a nest of deadly snakes without harm.

I know. You're wondering. Are any of these verses going to make a relatable point? Here it is:

Nothing will hurt or destroy in all my holy mountain, for as the waters fill the sea, so the earth will be filled with people who know the Lord.

Clearly, there are many fascinating things on this list—most of which point to God's insatiable desire to restore all things to a state of perfect peace. But the final item on the list—the one that sums it all up—is, again, the one most important thing.

As we approach the closing of time, and the Creator of all things closes the book on this world as we know it, there is absolutely nothing more important to Him than to be surrounded by an ocean of His beloved people. What kind of beloved people, you ask? Oh yeah, the kind of people who have real and true relationship with Him. Or as a fellow worship leader has said, REALationship.

It's simple. If your mother called from someone else's phone, you'd know her voice in two words. But if a stranger called you from an unknown number, you would have no idea. Similarly, we only come to know God's voice through continuous interaction with Him.

If you randomly met your favorite celebrity on the street for the first time—the one you know everything about, down to their shoe size—you'd still have to introduce yourself. Why? Because it's one thing to know *about* your favorite celebrity and quite another to actually *know* them.

Unfortunately, many people who attend church—even some in leadership—have this piddly type of relationship with God. They know all about His stories and His commands, what He loves and what He hates, even all the traditions of the church. But they honestly wouldn't know His voice if He shouted it from the rooftops.

God is going to have His way. He's going to acquire every item on His wish list. And He is, without a doubt, going to acquire for Himself an ocean of people who really do know Him. Who are truly awakened to His love. Why? Because this is His heart. Love. And it is the most important one thing there ever has been. Period.

NOTES

1.   Goll, *The Lost Art of Pure Worship*, 16.
2.   David Ferguson, *The Great Commandment Principle* (Wheaton, IL: Tyndale House, 1998).
3.   Goll, *The Lost Art of Pure Worship*, Endorsements.

CHAPTER 9

MADE FOR THIS

"Man is never more truly man than when he worships God."

—James B. Torrance

EVER WONDER WHAT you were made for?

Good question.

Of course, you know where I'm going with this. We've heard it all before. We were made for God. We were made for worship. We were made for His glory.

OK. Cool.

Is that so bad?

You see, something shifts tremendously inside of us when we realize our soul's purpose. We're changed when we finally embrace the truth that we were made for worship and worship was made for us. Revelation paints this picture extraordinarily:

> *Then I looked again, and I heard the voices of thousands and millions of angels around the throne and of the living beings and the elders. And they sang in a mighty chorus:*
>
> *"Worthy is the Lamb who was slaughtered—to receive power and riches and wisdom and strength and honor and glory and blessing."*

*And then I heard every creature in heaven and on earth and
under the earth and in the sea. They sang:*

*"Blessing and honor and glory and power belong to the one
sitting on the throne and to the Lamb forever and ever."*

*And the four living beings said, "Amen!" And the twen-
ty-four elders fell down and worshiped the Lamb* (Revelation 5:11-14).

Can you imagine it? All of creation doing exactly what we were
made to do? Gladly? All together? Willingly? All with one voice?
Joyfully? With one earth-shattering, spine-tingling, heart-pounding
sound? And not just a natural sound? But a spiritual sound? A uni-
fied spiritual sound?

It's ironic. Some fight it, saying, "But, what if I don't want to wor-
ship this God? What if I care to spend my energies another way?
What if I'm different? What if I don't find pleasure in worshiping
Him like everyone else?"

Okay. Reasonable questions.

But honestly, it's like asking, um, what if a dolphin doesn't feel
at home in the sea? Or what if a star prefers the idea of being a black
hole, or a mountain has audacious dreams of being a valley?

Why are we so offended by being told what we were made for? Why
does it irk us so much that God has created us for this one thing—to
worship Him and to honor Him with our lives above anything else?
To walk and talk with Him in fellowship? In intimate friendship?

It's odd.

We, ourselves, create and build things with a designated purpose all the time, and yet when it comes to us, we don't like it. Don't
understand it. Are disenfranchised by it.

Sure, most of us walk out the *action* part of worship just fine. Yet it's
the *subject matter* of worship that seems to create so much controversy.

Louie Giglio, in his book *The Air I Breathe*, records it this way: "I
don't know whether or not you consider yourself a 'worshiping' kind

of person, but you cannot help but worship—something. It's what you were made to do. Should you for some reason choose not to give God what He desires, you'll still worship something—exchanging the Creator for something He has created."[1]

Woah, that's a bold statement. Have you contemplated this before? It's not like we have a choice. To worship. We cannot simply refuse to worship. Sure, we can refuse to worship God, but if we don't worship God, the very choice we make to not worship Him becomes the choice we make to worship something else.

Therein lies one of the foremost reasons I am writing this book. If we struggle with this point—resist it at all—we prove we don't understand the heart of worship.

Consider this. The word *worship* literally means to ascribe worth to something; worth-ship. Giglio continues, "Worship is our response to what we value most. ...That 'thing' might be a relationship. A dream. Friends. Status. Stuff. A name. Some kind of pleasure. Whatever name you put on it, this thing or person is what you've concluded in your heart is worth most to you. And, whatever is worth most to you is—you guessed it—what you worship."[2]

Wait. Are we saying even those who identify as unbelievers—those who don't subscribe to the God of the Bible—are also worshipers? All the time? Even if they don't attend church?

Yep sir.

Why? Because we were born for this.

It's not a matter of being "religious" or not. It's not a matter of believing in God or not. It's simply a matter of fact. Everyone worships. Something.

There is no escape. We cannot turn off our worshiper DNA. It's wired in. Right into our motherboard. It's who we are. My friend, Jeff Grenell, quips, "We don't have to teach you how to worship. We just have to teach you how to worship God."

I love it!

See, our lives are already oozing with worship from our very first breath. Likely, some of it is directed toward God, while some of it is directed toward other things. There is worship already happening in each person's life—worship that is currently aimed at something or someone. Whether we know it or not.

The goal? To completely center our adoration and our lives on God. All of our time. Our energy. Our devotion. Our finances. Our resources. On God. To further His Kingdom. The Kingdom He invites us to enjoy with Him. In order that we walk in step with our foremost purpose. To live and breathe awakened worship.

> *There is worship already happening in each person's life—worship that is currently aimed at something or someone. Whether we know it or not.*

I know. This stinks. Depending on your perspective. It suggests we don't have a choice in the matter of whether or not we worship. But no. We do have a choice. Not in *whether* we worship, but in *who* or *what* we worship.

Not surprisingly, this is exactly where we so often fly off the tracks.

TASTE AND SEE

Worship, in its purest form, is simply the act of placing value on something or someone. We weigh in on the extent of our love for people, places, and things in the manner in which we emphasize them. In the way we spend our resources. Our time and money. Our emotions. Et cetera. We make these simple choices—to emphasize or not to emphasize—concerning every conceivable noun in every conceivable moment of our lives.

Obviously, when we choose to spend time or money on something, it does inherently mean that we cannot spend that same time or money on something else. We are therefore choosing to invest in that thing—in that moment—over all the other things in the universe. In doing so, we are assigning value to that thing and, in essence, are worshiping it.

Remarkably, Giglio takes things one step further by suggesting, "Whatever you worship, you become obsessed with. Whatever you become obsessed with, you imitate. And whatever you imitate, you become."[3]

What? We become what we worship?

Does this mean we become God when we worship God? No. Of course not. But we certainly begin to embody all of who He is—his character. Jack Hayford weighs in with his profound take; "Worship changes the worshiper into the image of the One worshiped."

Isn't this the goal? Yet it works conversely as well.

Psalm 115 makes its voice loud and clear concerning this idea.

> *Their idols are merely things of silver and gold, shaped by human hands. They have mouths but cannot speak, and eyes but cannot see. They have ears but cannot hear, and noses but cannot smell. They have hands but cannot feel, and feet but cannot walk, and throats but cannot make a sound. And those who make idols are just like them, as are all who trust in them* (Psalm 115:4-8).

Pause. Let it sink in.

Notice that last verse?

And those who make idols are just like them, as are all who trust in them.

Really?

How so?

Of course. It is true that every idol crafted by human hands has ears that can't hear and eyes that can't see. Not surprisingly, the psalmist isn't suggesting that those who worship idols will one day wake up to find themselves physically blind, deaf, or mute. No, he shifts effortlessly from speaking of physical sight and physical hearing to speaking of spiritual sight and spiritual hearing. He implies that when we engage in this type of idolatry, we will unavoidably find ourselves growing dull in our ability to see what God sees. To hear what

He hears. To sense what He senses. Spiritually. As we worship our idols. As we bow down to them. As we cling to their ways. As we are wooed by their false ideologies.

Think spiritual senses. We have five of them. Just as we have five physical senses. We can touch, see, hear, smell, and taste in the spirit. Yet when we worship idols, we become like them. So, if our idols are blind, we are blind. And so forth.

Spiritual seeing is understanding. So, when we become like non-seeing idols, we speak of losing our ability to understand the things of God—even the obvious things. Even the most trivial things. Some refer to this as 'feeling numb.'

Imagine. As we worship the things our own hands have made—that can neither walk nor talk—we become as they are. Spiritually lame. Spiritually crippled. Spiritually mute. Spiritually deaf. Spiritually handicapped. Utterly. Slowly. But surely.

Again. What are the characteristics of the idols mentioned in these verses? They have mouths that can't speak and eyes that can't see. Ears that can't hear and noses that can't smell. Hands that can't feel, and feet that can't walk.

This is terrifying!

Similarly, as John Piper describes, when we worship Jesus—the only true idol—we acquire His supernatural traits just the same. "From your heroes, you pick up mannerisms and phrases and tones of voice and facial expressions and habits and demeanors and convictions and beliefs. The more admirable the hero is and the more intense your admiration is, the more profound will be your transformation. In the case of Jesus, He is infinitely admirable, and our admiration rises to the most absolute worship. Therefore, when we behold Him as we should, the change is profound."

You see, worship is not something to be taken lightly. And worshiping idols is serious business. Why? Because we are, in essence, thumbing our noses at the One who made us. Yes. Worshiping idols of every kind—the wooden kind or the movie star kind—always comes at a price.

You may have wondered why it seems we've grown more and more confused over time as we absorb more and more arguments against the God-things we rarely questioned before. Some believe it's because we are becoming enlightened. But the truth is, it's because we are becoming "endarkened." Yep. Our spiritual seer is beginning to malfunction. Becoming hardened. Numb. Broken.

You can't help but wonder why it seems more difficult to hear God's voice than it used to be. It's no coincidence. It's not that we've finally arrived—finally woken up to the truth that God isn't real. No, it's that we are slowly—inch by inch—being lulled to sleep concerning the truth that God is real. Seriously? Yes. Because our spiritual sense of hearing has a way of becoming dulled. Covered. Plugged. And our spiritual sense of touch—the nerve endings connected to our spiritual feelers—has grown callused.

Have we begun to lose our taste for worship? For church? For studying the Bible? Yep. You guessed it. This means our spiritual taste buds are growing deadened toward the delicious delicacies of God, His Word, and His Spirit. Have we begun to grow increasingly torn between what is right and what is wrong? Maybe we've even become increasingly open to the idea that some of those "bad things" our parents originally forbade aren't really all that bad after all. I mean, it doesn't specifically say in the Bible not to...

Or it could be that our spiritual sense of smell—our discernment—is losing its edge, so that the aroma of God is being transformed ever so subtly into the putrid smell of fear, death, and doom. (See 2 Corinthians 2:15-16.) Could it be?

WE ARE WHAT WE EAT

First John 5:21 keeps it real. *"Dear children, keep away from anything that might take God's place in your hearts."*

I love to devour spoonsful of Ben and Jerry's ice cream. I do look forward to the weekends, when the Deyo household enjoys mixing in a few more delightful decadents to the dessert tray.

Half Baked. Tonight Dough. Milk and Cookies. Boom Chocolatta. Chocolate Therapy. Chocolate Peanut Buttery Swirl. Cookies and Cream Cheesecake Core. American Dream. Chunky Monkey.

Oh, so good. Oh, so tempting.

I suppose, based on Louie's conjecture, it is possible that I may—at any moment—spontaneously transform into a pint of Peanut Butter Cookie Core! Maybe. Maybe not. But you get the point.

There are many things pulling for our attention—for our worship—and we must recognize that worship is continuously rushing out of us whether we know it or not. Whether we like it or not. And for this reason, we must become increasingly intentional about placing our highest and greatest value on giving our worship to the One who gave it all for us.

And, why wouldn't we? Is Ben and Jerry's Chocolate Therapy ice cream capable of saving us from sin, death, or hell? Of reuniting us with our Father in Heaven? Of truly competing with the God of the Universe for fulfillment in our lives? If so, truly, we have not known Him. We have not sampled Him in the way we have sampled the other wonders of this exquisite world He created. We have not tasted and seen that He is good. Utterly good. That He is greater. That He soars infinitely above any other good thing. That there are depths of satisfaction and joy in God that we have yet to comprehend.

When we speak of worship this way—in the context of assigning value—we are not arguing the case that simply because I assign some value to Ben and Jerry's ice cream that I am now engaged in idol worship. If so, buying a new mattress from ComfyMattress.com would signify idolatry of the bedroom kind. (Granted, some of us do worship sleep, but that is another matter.)

Just because we take time to sit and eat our evening meal and therefore are unable to study our Bible in that moment, that does not mean we love food more than God. It is certainly possible to love food more than God and, in that sense, be engaged in idolatry of the gluttony kind. But we typically display this type of addiction by assigning excessive value to food or other things over time.

The point is, we must understand that God has created us to worship. It is an inherent part of our being that cannot be extracted. It is who we are. It is who we are supposed to be. It runs wildly through our veins. Yet, of course, He has created us to worship *Him*, first and foremost. It's who we were made to be. By Him. Yet, sadly many of us do not wish to function in the purpose for which we were made.

FUNCTION FUNK

It's fun to read about certain products in history that turned out to serve a vastly different purpose than the one they were created for.

Honestly, duct tape is one of the best examples. There's hardly anything that cannot be fixed—at least temporarily—with duct tape. Yet, how often is it actually used for taping ducts?

The Slinky was originally designed as a spring to help stabilize equipment on ships as they tossed and turned on the open sea. Fail? Not exactly. Millions have been sold for quite a different purpose.

Think Play-Doh.

In the 1930s, Kroger Grocery requested a product that could be sold and used in homes to remove the coal residue that would form on people's wallpaper as a result of the then popular coal-based heating. Nick McVicker created the pliable, putty-like substance for such a purpose. But, in the 1950s, as coal-based heating was replaced with natural gas, the product was reworked and marketed to Cincinnati-based schools. Nick's nephew, Joe McVicker, and his sister-in-law, nursery schoolteacher, Kay Zufall, came up with the name Play-Doh, and the new creative modeling clay was born!

It's crazy. Like many others, I didn't grow up with the understanding that I was made to worship God. Yes, I was a Christian.

And I went to church. But the truth about my true purpose escaped me.

Many of us search and search our whole lives to find purpose. We chase relationship after relationship hoping to discover it. We pour ourselves into our work hoping to find satisfaction. All the while, the world's best marketers scream at us to buy their products, claiming their latest merchandising innovations will help us reach the pinnacle of fulfillment through material things, entertainment, and pleasure.

Ironically, if we don't embrace this worldly propaganda, the Church often weighs in by appealing to our desire to chase after our dreams. For spiritual purposes. For ministry purposes. To be special. To have influence. To make a difference.

Ah, yes. That's it. The dream. Ultimately, it's the big dream that will usher fulfillment into our lives. And here we go again, circling back to the battle for purpose that rages between ministry and intimacy.

Don't we see it? Every voice of every generation is screaming at us to try to find contentment in something other than God. Someone other than God.

Listen. I'm not attempting to amputate the amoral things from our lives. God is pleased for us to enjoy all He has made. He created many things for our enjoyment. On the contrary, I'm hoping to reestablish that all things are spiritual. All things are meaningful. All things are worshipful. Yes, let us finally come to grips with the fact that everything we do is worship. In one way or another.

And this means we must respond in two simple ways. Commit ourselves to: 1) living every part of our lives unto God, including our playing, eating, working, and vacationing; 2) discontinuing all of the things in our lives that truly cannot be done unto the glory of God.

Can adultery be done to the glory of God? Can murder? Can gossip? Can lying or stealing? Of course not.

Can ice cream be eaten to the glory of God? Absolutely! In a certain moderation. Can we take a vacation to the glory of God? Yes.

Can playing or watching sports bring glory to God? Certainly. As we keep our priorities in line.

Ultimately, it is not a matter of whether these amoral things *can* be done unto God's glory. It is that they *must* be. And whatever things cannot be done unto His glory, must not be done at all.

We were made for worship and worship was made for us. Therefore, in joining with all the angels, the 24 elders, the living beings, and all of creation to worship the one true God, as described in Revelation 5, we fulfill our greatest and most fulfilling purpose. Each moment of every day.

NOTES

1.   Giglio, *The Air I Breathe*, 1.
2.   Ibid., 2.
3.   Ibid., 27.

CHAPTER 10

BECAUSE HE LOVES US

*"We don't worship God to gain his affection,
but because we already have it."*
—CHRIS DUPRÉ

ON NOVEMBER 2, 2002, John Mark McMillan wrote the song
"How He Loves." The previous night, he received a call—the kind of
phone call no one wants to get. His best friend had passed away from
complications to injuries he suffered in a car accident.

Stunned, John's heart was set on finding a way to process the pain
and yet—despite his frustration—he did not want to do so in a way
that pointed irate fingers at God. With a jumbled mess of disbelief,
sadness, and anger tumbling around on the inside, McMillan penned
these words for his friend. For himself. For all of us.

*He is jealous for me
Loves like a hurricane, I am a tree
Bending beneath the weight of His wind and mercy
When all of a sudden
I am unaware of these afflictions eclipsed by glory
And I realize just how beautiful You are
And how great Your affections are for me
Oh, how He loves us so
Oh, how He loves us*

How He loves us so
We are His portion, and He is our prize
Drawn to redemption by the grace in His eyes
If His grace is an ocean, we're all sinking
And Heaven meets earth like a sloppy wet kiss
And my heart turns violently inside of my chest
I don't have time to maintain these regrets
When I think about the way
He loves us
Oh, how He loves us
Oh, how He loves us
Oh, how He loves

HE FIRST

As we seek to peel back the layers underneath the *why* of worship—to uncover its intrinsic and intoxicating purpose—the most compelling reason I've found is *He first*.

I am still impacted greatly by a message I heard IHOP co-founder, Mike Bickle, speak while I was leading worship at a conference in Nashville years ago. It was the first time I had ever heard someone present this "He first" theology. A theology which puts forth the stunning notion that God has never asked us to do anything He has not already done Himself.

Whether it's living, giving, loving, or dying, He refuses to set before us tasks to accomplish or rules to follow that He has not already fulfilled.

It's true. God asks us to love others—even to love our "enemies." Yet He has not asked us to do so without first doing so Himself. How so? First, we know He has unequivocally offered every person on the earth the free gift of salvation. Regardless of their love for Him. *"He died for everyone so that those who receive his new life will no longer live for themselves. Instead, they will live for Christ, who died and was raised for them"* (2 Cor. 5:15).

Furthermore, though we rarely imagine ourselves as enemies of God, the Bible differs on the matter. In Colossians 1:20-21, Paul reminds us that God made peace with everything in heaven and on earth by means of Christ's blood on the cross. *"This includes you who were once far away from God. You were his enemies, separated from him by your evil thoughts and actions."*

Paul continues to perplex: *"Yet now he has reconciled you to himself through the death of Christ in his physical body. As a result, he has brought you into his own presence, and you are holy and blameless as you stand before him without a single fault"* (Col. 1:22).

The most compelling verse? *"But God showed his great love for us by sending Christ to die for us while we were still sinners"* (Rom. 5:8).

While we were still sinners. While we were still in bondage to our great rebellion. While we were still His enemies.

The notion of "He first" continues painlessly in its application to giving. As a foundational Kingdom principle, God calls us to give—our hearts, our money, our time, our trust, etc. But again, He doesn't require this of us without first operating daringly in it Himself by giving us everything we possess—not the least of which is His one and only Son. (I started to make a list of the things He has given us, but thought better of it, realizing you would understand the term *everything* without me providing oodles of examples.)

The same is true for love. The popular First John 4:19 illuminates this idea when it proclaims, *"We love each other because he loved us first."*

He originates. We reciprocate.

What a stunning exposé.

You probably realized this, but we aren't the ones who initiated this thing called worship. We aren't the ones who loved first. We aren't the ones who gave first. We aren't the ones who moved heaven and earth to reestablish broken relationship. We aren't the ones who took the first steps. No. He has taken an infinite number of steps toward us as a means of coaxing us to take even a few steps toward Him. That He might march us straight into His loving arms.

When He asks us to worship Him, He is no fool. He recognizes He has already proven His love for us even while making His grand request. He readily knows, as established earlier, that beseeching us to love Him only requires that we reciprocate a love He has grandly instigated. One that begs we respond with the words, "I love you, too, Lord."

A SINGING AND SPINNING GOD

No analogy is perfect, but this "He first" one tends to go the distance.

What about submission? Did God actually model submission before asking us to submit to Him? Of course. He did so perfectly through the life of Jesus. His Son effectively modeled for us what it looks like to willingly and obediently say and do only what His Father said and did. Nothing more. Nothing less. The same can be said of God's invitation for us to join Him in so many other areas. Like suffering, dying to self, overcoming temptation, resisting the devil, acting in faith, spiritual warfare, etc.

He first.

Believe it or not, this concept even extends over into worship— more than most would think. To comprehend, we'll need to take another look at a verse I presented in Chapter 6: *"For the Lord your God is living among you. He is a mighty savior. He will take delight in you with gladness. With his love, he will calm all your fears. He will rejoice over you with joyful songs"* (Zeph. 3:17).

It's slightly overwhelming to ponder the idea that God sings. Can you hear it? Can you envision such a moment? Where the heavens open up and out comes this voice? This dreadfully wonderful voice. It makes me shudder to think. If God opened His mouth and allowed us to hear Him. Audibly. Oh, the terror. Oh, the beauty.

Oh, the irony. That this little gem is hidden safely in one of the books of the minor prophets for all of us crazy God-seekers to dig up, possibly during of a time of great personal trial. Incredible.

You may have imagined I was stretching this "He first" idea a little too far. Like all creative writers, right? You may still. But I'm not.

"Yes," you say. "God loves us. But seriously. He doesn't literally partake in the other elements of our traditional worship services—like singing? Or dancing?"

Um, yep, He does. He really did get the proverbial ball rolling. He really did tip over the very first domino. As explained, He sang proudly and lovingly over us long before inviting us to lift our voices to Him. Not only that. The word *rejoice* in the last segment of Zephaniah 3:17—where it says *"He will rejoice over you with joyful songs"*—is actually the Hebrew word *giyl*, pronounced "gheel." Its meaning is outlined by *Strong's Dictionary* this way: "A primitive root; properly, to spin round (under the influence of any violent emotion), i.e. usually rejoice, or (as cringing) fear—be glad, joy, be joyful, rejoice."[1]

So in other words, just as God has not been caught inviting us to sing without first opening His mouth, He has not invited us to dance without first doing so Himself. (This too is one of those lessons I was learning way back when—during my early Sonicflood days—from an incredible friend and mentor, Ray Hughes.)

Dance? God? Seriously? Yes! It's easy to see from this little Hebrew word *giyl* that God, our God—the one true, omnipotent God—is *spinning around under the influence of violent joy* in His great love for His people. Dancing like a fool, because He loves us. And oh, how He loves us!

RESPONSE TO REVELATION

There is something ridiculous that happens to us when we realize we don't *have* to love God but that we *get* to love God. That loving God is honestly less like a command and more like an invitation. Don't miss this. If we can make an epic attitude tweak in this one area concerning worship—and other challenges we face—it will change our lives forever.

One of the more prevailing themes connected to corporate worship has been best branded *revelation and response*. This idea is typically realized when authentic, impactful, transformational worship (our response to God) flows out of Holy Spirit-inspired, supernatural eye-openers (God's revelation to us). Or you could say it this way: a worshipful response *to* God is always born out of an insightful revelation *from* God.

To me, this concept is extremely rudimentary but still, oh, so profound.

> A worshipful response to God is always born out of an insightful revelation from God.

In an interview discussing his book *Facedown*, Matt Redman explains, "I think all true meaningful and pure worship is a response to a revelation. One way I like to define worship is 'the all-consuming response to the all-deserving worth and revelation of God.' When we see him, it commands a response to his holiness. Worship starts with us seeing him."[2]

Yes! Yes! And this, of course, only stands to strengthen the notion that we love because He first loved us.

It also begs the question. How can you—how can I—love a God we do not know? A God we have not *seen*? A God of whom we have no understanding? No revelation? It's like saying "I do" to someone after shaking their hand for the first time on a blind date. There's no basis for commitment. What could you possibly commit to?

Still, many leaders mistakenly characterize corporate worship as something that only paves the way for greater revelation—for the preaching of the Word—nothing more and nothing less. But let's take another look. Yes, worship can pave the way for the preaching of the Word. But not exclusively. The truth is connected—oddly enough—to the seemingly arbitrary question of the chicken and the egg. You know. Which comes first? Response or revelation?

Stay with me.

Because we know God created adult humans first, not babies, and because we know He created animals in their adult state as well, we can assume He created the chicken first. Not the egg. Right?

Capeesh? (Sorry to spoil that for ya.)

Anywho.

It is illogical to assume that response comes first. Before revelation. Response to what? Response to God? In the form of worship? How can we respond to nothing? How can we love or worship a God who is unknown to us? Impossible.

God must first awaken something in us toward His existence. Toward His glory. Toward His power. Toward our need for Him. Toward our need for a Savior.

> For no one can come to me unless the Father who sent me draws them to me, and at the last day I will raise them up. As it is written in the Scriptures, "They will all be taught by God." Everyone who listens to the Father and learns from him comes to me (John 6:44-45).

Think back. To the day you realized your own great need for a Savior. You didn't truly worship Him before that day, did you? But, now—in response to an incredible revelation received through the Word of God and/or the Spirit of God—you fall to your knees, repent, and cry holy, all in a flurry of response. To a supernatural revelation.

Worship doesn't start with a response. It starts with a revelation. The revelation that *He first* loved us. That *He first* gave of Himself. That *He first* bridged the gap. That *He first* broke through time and space, shoved Himself into a tiny, human-skin suit, if only to reveal something we could never conceive on our own. Something that should startle even the most jaded among us. Something that has inspired billions of people around the globe—throughout all of history—to join together in one song with one voice. Not because they have to. But because there is no other fitting response. To the revelation of His reckless love.

NOTES

1.   James Strong, *Strong's Exhaustive Concordance of the Bible*, H1523.

2.   Danielle DuRant, "A Conversation with Matt Redman," RZIM, November 1, 2004, http://rzim.org/just-thinking/a-conversation-with-matt-redman/.

CHAPTER 11

PROTECTION IN HIS PRESENCE

"Safety comes in our nearness to God, not in our distance from our enemies."

—DILLON BURROUGHS

MANY IN OUR day are full of fear. Seems like more than any other time in history. Strangely enough. Yet, I imagine we could argue, for good reason. ISIS. Suicide bombers. Wars. Attacks. Assault weapons. Snipers. Stabbings. Calamites. Accidents. Disease. Natural disasters. And the list goes on.

Reading in Psalm 27 recently, I came across a fairly basic yet important biblical principle that yearns to shed light on the abundant benefits that are ours in connection with this thing we call worship.

There is protection in God's presence.

Now, I realize this could seem relatively uninteresting, or cliché, or something, but I'm thinking we shouldn't knock the notion of divine protection—of any sort—especially while living in an era when many feel highly vulnerable to tragedy. It's true, right? It seems we've never lived in a time when people are more afraid—with the rise of assaults, school shootings, weaponized vehicles, major venue explosions, police shootings, racial violence, murders, floods, fires, earthquakes, tsunamis, hurricanes, tornadoes, and more! And still, we tend to yawn when someone suggests the answer could be found in the protection of God's powerful presence. Interesting.

As I mentioned in Chapter 5, I've been discerning that we do underestimate God's presence—perceiving it simply as a type of ushy-gushy, feel-good emotion, accessible only during our Sunday sing-alongs, rather than truly grasping the incredible opportunity we are provided to live safeguarded in His presence each moment of every day.

Remember: God's presence isn't something out there. Something intangible. Something I hope to lure into my song service. If I sing loud enough or dance wildly enough. It is *Him*. His person. It is not a glory cloud or a fierce emotion or even an "it." *He* is "It." And it is Him I seek. God Himself. My God. My King. My Friend. Truly, when we say we have encountered God's presence, we are suggesting we have come face to face with Him, His person, His being.

THE HIDDEN PLACE

In continuing with this theme, we can say that when we are with Him, in His presence—engaged in relationship and walking and talking with Him daily—there are many blessings that go far beyond the goose bumps.

The familiar part of Psalm 27:4 reads like this: *"The one thing I ask of the Lord—the thing I seek most—is to live in the house of the Lord all the days of my life, delighting in the Lord's perfections and meditating in his Temple."* I shared this verse in Chapter 8.

But as tempted as we might be to stop here, let's read on.

> *For he will conceal me there when troubles come, he will hide me in his sanctuary. He will place me out of reach on a high rock* (Psalm 27:5).

He will conceal me *there* when troubles come.

But *where* is *there?* Of course, *there* is in God's Temple, in His sanctuary, on a high rock. Beyond the reach of true troubles. Just as the text reveals. Of course, these particular places are not literal, physical places but symbols representing an incredible, spiritual place. A hidden place. A safe place. A place out of reach of our true enemies. Out of reach of *the* enemy.

This is the place where we find ourselves "wasting time" delighting in His perfections and meditating on His Word and on His ways. It's the place where we find ourselves abiding in Christ and fellowshipping with the Father. The secret place. The relationship place. The healing place. The revelation place. The intimate place. The shielded place. The place especially designed for me and my God. For you and your God. For us and our God.

This is the spiritual space where we are divinely protected. Where we are divinely sheltered. Where we are divinely secure. In God.

This is fantastic news, but...

We must ask, do we find ourselves regularly in this place? Honestly?

We certainly find ourselves seeking security and safety. Often. We undoubtedly desire a place where we are truly free from attack and strife. From bigotry and prejudice. From slander and persecution. But I wonder, do we often find ourselves seeking security and safety apart from seeking the One who embodies these things on our behalf?

It's not simply that God *provides* safety and security like some cosmic vending machine. No. He *is* safety and security. He doesn't just *provide* protection. He *is* protection. And when we seek Him— and fellowship with Him—we abide in all that He is. Including His divine protection.

We may not grasp it, but there is great distinction between having something and being something. To quote my friend, Jeremy Johnson, "When you *have* something, it can be taken away, but when you *are* something, nothing in hell can change that fact." God does not simply know the source of our protection. He does not simply point us in the direction of the source. He *is* the source. Of all good things. And all good things emanate from His being.

If we seek protection and safety apart from God, it is accurate to say we will never find them. They will constantly escape us. But when we seek God first—His presence, relationship with Him, refuge in Him—then protection and safety are part of the package deal.

> It's not that God provides safety and security like some kind of cosmic vending machine. No. He is safety and security.

So many are running to and fro attempting to create safety. Endeavoring to find an asylum. Even attempting to sell security. Fretting, seemingly having lost sight of where our true protection comes from. Desperately wondering if it can be found in a president or a company. In wealth, in success, or in power. In a relationship, in a degree, or in an achievement. Even in technology.

Yet it eludes us.

LIVING IN HIS SHADOW

Psalm 31:19-20 announces, *"How great is the goodness you have stored up for those who fear you. You lavish it on those who come to you for protection, blessing them before the watching world. You hide them in the shelter of your presence, safe from those who conspire against them. You shelter them in your presence, far from accusing tongues."*

Here we see the connection between the fear of the Lord and relationship with God as well as the benefits of protection in His presence.

Isn't it unsettling to note how we've looked to insufficient human remedies to calm our fears rather than to the all-sufficient supernatural power and presence of Jesus? Isaiah 8:13 announces that God alone is to be feared, clarifying that when we fear Him, we need not fear anything else!

Are there logical reasons to be afraid in these times? Absolutely. Many. If we're living in the natural, with terrorists and shooters and bombs and guns, it is entirely *logical* to be restlessly glancing over our shoulder wherever we go. It is entirely *logical* to be nervous about going to large public gatherings or taking public transportation. But we are not living in the natural. In the logical. We are not subject to the same horrors that those who rebel against the Lord are. We are recreated beings living not in the natural or in the logical, but in the supernatural. Hidden in the shadow of His wings.

Cue the eye roll.

But seriously!

There are much greater reasons to be afraid if we are intent on looking solely to human leaders, military powers, or political parties to protect us rather than to God. The One who created those in power. If we are found daily living in His presence, we simply need not be afraid. Think of it. The greatest of the world's leaders—combined—truly have nothing to offer us in and of themselves. Nothing outside of what God has given them. Whatever strength they have is only that which has emanated from the source—*the* Source. And their strength is but a fraction of His own.

To be sure, we are not saying that being under the covering of God's presence makes us immune to difficult circumstances or attack. Yet we are saying that God will protect us in the midst of anything we face. I love the response of Shadrach, Meshach, and Abed-Nego when King Nebuchadnezzar threatened to throw them into the fiery furnace. They said simply, *"Our God whom we serve is able to deliver us from the burning fiery furnace, and He will deliver us from your hand, O king. But if not, let it be known to you, O king, that we do not serve your gods, nor will we worship the gold image which you have set up"* (Dan. 3:17-18 NKJV).

They respectfully declared that their God was able to deliver them, and they even said, "He will deliver us." But then they uttered these powerful words; "But if not." And this is the attitude we must adopt with God. We believe and trust regardless.

Serving God is not all butterflies and rainbows. Most of the apostles died horrible deaths as martyrs. Jesus Himself told His disciples—and us—that as believers we should expect to face many difficulties in this life. *"These things I have spoken to you, that in Me you may have peace. In the world you will have tribulation; but be of good cheer, I have overcome the world"* (John 16:33 NKJV).

NO OTHER SHELTER

Crazy as it sounds, there is no real protection beyond His presence. Even unbelievers who remain protected do so as a result of God's divine protection, whether they acknowledge it or not. Yet this is our remedy? We look to earthy powers to solve heavenly issues? It's like we've completely lost sight of obvious biblical truths. Remember?

> *Though a thousand fall at your side, though ten thousand are dying around you, these evils will not touch you* (Psalm 91:7).

> *I lay down and slept, yet I woke up in safety, for the Lord was watching over me. I am not afraid of ten thousand enemies who surround me on every side* (Psalm 3:5-6).

> *He takes no pleasure in the strength of a horse or in human might. No, the Lord's delight is in those who fear him, those who put their hope in his unfailing love* (Psalm 147:10-11).

> *The foolish plan of God is wiser than the wisest of human plans, and God's weakness is stronger than the greatest of human strength* (1 Corinthians 1:25).

> *It is better to take refuge in the Lord than to trust in people. It is better to take refuge in the Lord than to trust in princes* (Psalm 118:8-9).

> *Some nations boast of their chariots and horses, but we boast in the name of the Lord our God. Those nations will fall down and collapse, but we will rise up and stand firm* (Psalm 20:7-8).

Reread. Meditate. Apply.

So, what about it? Where will we live? With one foot firmly planted in the logic of man and one tentatively planted in the power of God? Putting futile hope in the ways of this world and measily hope in the ways of God? Looking partially to the wisdom of the sons of men and partially to the wisdom of the Son of God? Just in case?

Why?

Truly, there is no wisdom that emanates from the heart of man apart from God. Any knowledge that man possesses is but a fragment of the comprehensive knowledge of God, acquired only by the grace and mercy of God. Truly, there is no protection or prosperity or production or provision that can originate from man apart from God. Everything is found in Him. In connection with Him. In His presence.

Do you desire safety in these dangerous times? *Find yourself in His presence.*

Do you long for security in a world where fears cripple and thieves break in? *Find yourself in His presence.*

Do you seek protection from those who would use and abuse you? From circumstances beyond your control? From hurt, rejection, loss, and disappointment? *Find yourself in His presence.*

Why worship? Why lose yourself moment by moment in His presence? Why draw close to your Father in heaven in the secret place and all throughout the day?

Because there is no other shelter. There is no other refuge. There is no other hope. There is no other joy. These treasures are found only in God's eternal, everlasting, all-pervading presence.

SECTION 3

WHO AGAIN ARE WE WORSHIPING?

CHAPTER 12

THE INVISIBLE VISIBLE GOD

*"If our knowledge of God is superficial,
our worship will be superficial."*
—R.C. Sproul

THIS CHAPTER, ALONG with the next, are probably the two most critical chapters in this book. And the most in-depth. Not surprisingly, if we manage to awaken to the *what*, *why*, and *how* of worship and yet miss the *who*, we'll likely remain in our deadened—or "dead-end"—state toward pure worship. Toward awakened REALationship with God.

For this reason, we're going to take a much closer look at the three persons of God—the Father, the Son, and the Holy Spirit—in order to more fully understand their roles and how they function together and, as a result, discover the best ways to interact with them in relationship. (Please don't skip over this portion just because you are a seasoned leader/believer. There are important revelations here that will surprise and challenge you. Especially when it comes to the role of Jesus.)

It may seem obvious, but as much as we use the names God, Jesus, Father, Lord, and others interchangeably, the three persons of God are very different—and yet very much the same. Both and. They are truly one being, yet they serve distinctly different roles. For this reason, it is our joy to search out and discover over a lifetime—truly, over all of eternity—just exactly who they are. It's the same process we enjoy as we grow closer and closer to a spouse or a best friend over time, peeling back layer after layer of their personality, of their passions, of their being, year after year, encounter after encounter, day after day, experience after experience.

So, who is God?

Can we really know Him?

Is Jesus the central focal point of Christianity?

Should we pray to Jesus?

What role does the Holy Spirit play?

Should we worship the Holy Spirit?

Has anyone ever seen the Father? Will we see Him in heaven?

Should we seek relationship with the Father, the Son, or the Holy Spirit? Or all three? How does this work?

Am I even asking the right questions?

I love wrestling with these and other intriguing issues.

Let's begin with this passage.

> *For, at just the right time Christ will be revealed from heaven by the blessed and only almighty God, the King of all kings and Lord of all lords. He alone can never die, and he lives in light so brilliant that no human can approach him. No human eye has ever seen him, nor ever will. All honor and power to him forever! Amen* (1 Timothy 6:15-16).

Praise the Lord. This is almost too much! Read that again. Seriously. Maybe five or six times over. Pause and ponder. Worship Him. Right in this moment.

Selah.

We glean many things from this scripture, not the least of which is that God, Himself, cannot—and will not—ever be seen. Only Jesus. Understandably, this may be something we have to process for a minute. (Or 25.) Something we haven't seriously contemplated, before. If we're honest.

Of course, this scripture doesn't establish itself on an island. The Apostle John proclaims, *"No one has ever seen God. But the unique One [Jesus], who is himself God, is near to the Father's heart. He has revealed God to us* (John 1:18).

There we go. *Ever* pretty much covers it.

Jesus' own words echo a similar sentiment in John 6:46: *"Not that anyone has ever seen the Father; only I, who was sent from God, have seen him."* (I realize there are passages where men like Moses and Abraham are said to have seen God, but in those instances, it is fairly clear that they are meeting with the Lord, Jesus—not God, the Father. You may need to do more study on this, but this is the most realistic manner in which these Old Testament and New Testament passages can coexist.)

Okay, so God cannot—and will not—be seen by us with our eyes. But can He be known? Yes. Of course. Through Christ. And through His Spirit. In fact, this is God's greatest desire. To be known. By us. In relationship. As I've mentioned time and again in this book.

This is precisely why He has revealed Himself by sending us His Son, Jesus. One we could see.

> *Christ is the visible image of the invisible God. He existed before anything was created and is supreme over all creation* (Colossians 1:15).

It's straightforward. God is invisible. But He is made visible to us through Christ. If we want to know what He is like—who God is— we can be assured that when we see Jesus, we have seen the Father. Fully. Not in part. But in whole.

Yet in seeming contradiction, we are invited by our beautiful Savior in John 16:23 to skip the middle man and go directly to the Father—because He loves us dearly.

Wow. Let's dig a little deeper.

THE WAY TO THE FATHER

I had just finished leading worship at a conference a few years back when Jose Duran got up to speak. I didn't know him at the time, but he has since become a friend. He opened with a few personal pleasantries and then asked something that floored me. "Is it possible in our Church culture that we have overemphasized Jesus?"

What?

Is this guy cuckoo for Cocoa Puffs, or what? Really? Is he serious? I mean how can anybody overemphasize Jesus? He is the center of it all. Everything we stand for is built upon the foundation of who Jesus is and what He has done for us. For crying out loud. The entire Bible—every single book—laser points straight to Jesus. Straight to the all-encompassing provision He makes for us through His death and resurrection.

Honestly, this was one of the first times in a long time I had sat in a service convinced that the preacher had lost it. Completely. I was done. Ready to tune out.

Then he read John 14:6: *"Jesus told him [Thomas], 'I am the way, the truth, and the life. No one can come to the Father except through me.'"*

Further proof of this guy's lunacy, right?

Maybe. Maybe not.

This often-quoted verse centers entirely on Jesus, right? Of course. For sure.

Or does it?

Jesus is the *way*. Jesus is the *truth*. Jesus is the *life*. There. It's settled. Jesus is the center of it all! Wait a minute. We should write a song—"Jesus is the center of it all...." Oh, someone did that already. Right. Right. I digress.

Anyway. As Jose continued to preach, try as I might, I couldn't tune him out. And the further he went, the more I discovered I didn't want to.

He posed a simple question. If Jesus is the way—and we all know He is—than what exactly is He the way to? Life? Liberty? Happiness? What?

Good question.

THE PURPOSE OF THE WAY

As he preached, Jose laid out this neat little metaphor. Imagine I was planning a road trip to Disney with my family. For me, this would be an extensive journey since we live in Minneapolis, Minnesota. Amongst the frozen chosen.

I would simply open my simple-to-use smartphone map app and plug in the starting and ending points. Then I'd look at the overall trip. Big picture. The time needed. The roads we'd travel. The potential stops. Et cetera. Then, after cramming all of our travel gear into the happy-family minivan—including my brand-new, cherry-red, polka dot swimwear (not really)—we'd pile in and hit the road.

But wouldn't it be strange if we never got to Disney? Because we were too preoccupied with the road? What if we drove up and down the highway and never actually reached our intended destination? What if we couldn't help but stop every five miles to see the sites and to kiss the pavement? Backtracking time and again. Overjoyed beyond imagination that someone, somewhere took the time to build a road to help us get to Disney.

It wouldn't be all bad. I mean, roads can be nice. Roads are certainly essential. Driving on roads is often fun. And, of course, if roads didn't exist, there could be—there would be—no getting to Disney. Without the road, there would be no road trip. And there would be little chance of reaching our destination.

Okay. I was beginning to catch on. Starting to see where this guy was going, and yet I remained largely cynical.

He continued. "Ask yourself again. If Jesus is the way—the road, the path on which we travel—what is He the way to? Where is He leading us? And what or who is the destination?"

Now, before we get too excited, let's go back to the passage. What exactly does John 14:6 say? Read it again. Slowly. *"Jesus told him [Thomas], 'I am the way, the truth and the life. No one can come to the Father except through me.'"*

It's baffling, because it's right there. I didn't see it, and I've read it like 1,000 times. I've heard it quoted 10,000 times! Go on. Read the second half of the verse. It doesn't mince words.

"No one can come to the Father except through me."

Still don't see it?

Let's take an alternate route.

What is the ultimate goal communicated in this verse? What is the ultimate truth in Jesus' statement? Why exactly is it that we need to be made aware of the fact that Jesus is the way? The truth? The life? Why? To give us a useful description of Jesus? To win the argument we have with other religions over how to get to heaven? Or...to make us aware of the incredible fact that we've been provided a ticket? A ticket to somewhere special? Somewhere we could never go without the unbelievable sacrifice of Jesus?

There it is. I gave it away. The singular purpose found in John 14:6 is forthright—yet it is often lost on us. Jesus left heaven, came to earth, and then died and rose again for one important solitary reason. To open a way for us—where there was no way—that we might attain full access to a very special destination.

And what is that destination?

Disney?

No.

Jesus?

No.

The Holy Spirit?

No.

Heaven?

Emphatically, no!

The Father?

Yes. That's what the verse says.

"No one can **come to the Father** *except through me."*

There we go. Because of this verse (and many others) we can undoubtedly conclude that one of the primary and most wonderful goals in life—as stated by and made possible through Jesus—is to find our way to the Father.

When taken a step further, we can also conclude that the manner or *way* in which we get to the Father is not the end goal. This is big. The *way* is a wonderful means, but it is not the end. Getting to the Father is the end. The end of all ends. The one most important thing.

Ironically, this is the very thing that Jesus ultimately pursued for Himself as well as for all of us while walking the earth—getting back to the Father. (Not that He ever truly left the Father, but you understand. There was a distinct breech in relationship between them while Jesus hung on that cross—a time when the Father forsook Jesus for our sake.) Then, following His death and resurrection, He left earth. Why? So the Holy Spirit would come to help us *and* so He could return to His Father's right hand. The place where He and we belong.

The greatest aspiration Jesus has for all people—above all others—is to be one with the Father. Just as He and the Holy Spirit are. This is awakened pure worship. This is life's ultimate prize.

Even still, we typically refuse to see the Father as the primary focus in this verse. Blink and you'll miss it. If you're not paying attention even right in this moment. This false narrative has been so ingrained in the Church that it can be hardly removed.

Jesus is the one speaking in John 14:6, and He is desperately trying to tell us something so very important. And we think we hear Him.

But because of centuries of misguided teaching, we largely assume Jesus—the Way—is the chief end. But no. Coming to the Father. To be *with* Him, to have fellowship with Him (along with Jesus and the Holy Spirit). This is the true end. The end-all, be-all.

I realize there can be some added confusion about all this, especially since we are generally acutely aware of the truth that Jesus is God, and God is Jesus, and so forth. Yet, we've become so accustomed to using their names interchangeably that we forget Jesus and His Father—though they are absolutely one—do have entirely different roles to play. Just as the Spirit does.

THE JUICE

In our metaphor with Disney, we've established that Jesus is the way—the road. God the Father is the destination. So where does this leave the Holy Spirit?

Simple.

The Holy Spirit is the fuel.

Huh?

You and I are the car. Sitting on the road (the Way). Now, without the road, it is entirely impossible to get to the destination. (Off-roading just won't cut it.) And just to clarify, if you missed it. Heaven is *not* the destination. The Father is the destination. Heaven is like the acreage Disney sits on. The dirt. It houses the precious cargo of heaven, but it is not nearly as important as what it houses. Namely, fellowship with the Father.

Can I say it again? Heaven is not the end goal. Granted, heaven is a wonderful place, but it's not wonderful because it is heaven. It's wonderful because it's where the Father is.

Interestingly, when faced with the uncertainty of life after death, the whole world is enamored mostly with whether or not they'll make it to heaven. Why? Because we often wrongly assume the point of accepting Jesus as Lord and Savior is to avoid hell and make heaven.

Ironically, the assumption that heaven is the end goal erases the one most important reason Jesus died as well as the one main focus of the Holy Spirit as He works in our lives—to bring us back to the Father.

That said, our car could be sitting nicely on the road, with the pathway laid out before us (provided by the incredible sacrifice of Jesus on the cross). We're there, belted in, totally stoked about the trip, when all of a sudden, we realize we've got no fuel. No power. No juice.

So, with all our might, we attempt to pick up our car and drag it toward the destination. Come on! What's the problem? Jesus made a way. A way where there was no way. The *only* way.

We can almost see the destination off in the distance. Surely, we can inch our way there with a little willpower. But alas, we find ourselves stuck, creeping at a pace that's slower than a snail in molasses. We'll never make it.

Finally we wise up and look to a greater power than will power. We receive the baptism of the Holy Spirit and immediately start cruising. We're on our way. To the Father. Via the Spirit. On the pathway Jesus laid out for us by conquering death, hell, and the grave. Yes!

DEMOTING JESUS

But before you stone me, Jose and I are not in any way attempting to demote Jesus. Not possible. Jesus is beyond essential to the equation. He gets it. He knows His incomparable role. And He plays it perfectly. The question is, do we? Fact is. Without Jesus, it is impossible to get to the Father. One hundred percent. It's just not going to happen. Yet, the fact remains. Our main goal is not to get to Jesus. But to get to the Father. Through Jesus. In the power of the Holy Spirit.

Think of it this way. There was a door. Locked. Shut. With no access. Standing between you and God. God and Jesus have relationship together with the Holy Spirit. But there's a dilemma. They want you and me to join them. So, Jesus makes a great sacrifice to open the door to us through His torturous death on the cross. He steals the keys from the devil, comes back to life, and voila! The locks are busted and the door is blown clean off. Access to the Father is granted through the one true Door, Jesus.

I am the door. If anyone enters by Me, he will be saved, and will go in and out and find pasture (John 10:9 NKJV).

At the risk of being redundant, can I ask again? Is the Door the goal? Of course not. The Door is a passageway. To the goal. Without the Door, access to the Father cannot be granted. It's only when we enter through the Door into the lush green pastures of awakened relationship with God that we discover what we were made for. Communion with the Father.

Though the Father, the Son, and the Holy Spirit have distinct roles, they have the same goal.

Please understand. This type of talk does not belittle Jesus in the slightest. In fact, we truthfully honor Jesus' sacrifice best by doing what He meant for us to do—by running passionately through that door to boldly enter into intimate, awakened relationship with God.

Now all of us, whether Jews or Gentiles, may come to God the Father with the Holy Spirit's help because of what Christ has done for us (Ephesians 2:18 TLB).

Fellowship with the Father—in perfect unity with the Son and the Holy Spirit. It's what Adam and Eve had. It's what they lost. And it's what all of heaven is making possible once again.

CHAPTER 13

AN UNEQUIVOCALLY SUPREME GOD

"The Son will put himself under God's authority, so that God, who gave his Son authority over all things, will be utterly supreme over everything everywhere."

—THE APOSTLE PAUL

IF GOD IS supreme over all, how do the three persons of God—Father, Son, and Spirit—navigate this power "struggle?"

Interesting question.

Honestly, people get a little freaked out when we start talking about the Trinity. God the Father. God the Son. And God the Spirit. It's a little heady. I admit. But it's also central to our understanding of awakened worship, because we must fully grasp *who* we're worshiping if we're truly going to fulfill God's purpose with our lives.

Of course, we always have the egg analogy. There are three parts to every egg. White, yolk, and shell. Each is a different and distinct part of the egg, yet each is equally included as part of the egg. We would never reason that the shell is not part of the egg, but we would also never say the shell serves the same function as the yolk. Or the white.

Three in one.

We also have the classic H_2O analogy. There are three states to water. Solid, liquid, and gas. Each is a different and distinct form of water, yet each is labeled by the same elements on the periodic table. Ice is still H_2O. Liquid is still H_2O. Steam is still H_2O. Solid. Liquid. Gas. Three in one.

Truth is. It's not too difficult to understand the idea that the three persons of God have different roles. Yet we shouldn't miss the fact that though the Father, the Son, and the Holy Spirit have distinct roles, they have the same goal.

How does Jesus play into this? Let's take a closer look.

AWAKENED TO THE SON

Let's start with this question; where is Jesus?

Paul cuts to the chase.

> *God raised Jesus from the dead, and we are all witnesses of this. Now he is exalted to the place of highest honor in heaven, at God's right hand. And the Father, as he had promised, gave him the Holy Spirit to pour out upon us, just as you see and hear today* (Acts 2:32-33).

Clearly, Jesus is not the person of God on the planet any longer. After 33 years of ministry, He has—in a manner of speaking— peaced-out and returned to the Father's side, sending us the Spirit of God to fill and empower the sons of men.

With this in mind—with worship in mind—let us be reawakened to a few essentials concerning who Jesus is:

- The Word Incarnate.
- The Spotless Lamb.
- The Lion of the Tribe of Judah.
- High Priest Forever.
- Our Brother.
- Savior and Lord.

John lays it out. *"So the Word became human and made his home among us. He was full of unfailing love and faithfulness. And we have seen his glory, the glory of the Father's one and only Son"* (John 1:14).

When we say that Jesus is the Word Incarnate we are saying something truly mysterious! That God—through His Son, Jesus—became human while maintaining His divine nature, essentially taking on two natures. Both God and man. One hundred percent God. One hundred percent man.

While this is deeply perplexing, it is also completely wonderful! Only God can be Holy, yet for His plan of redemption to succeed, He would require a human who could fulfill His laws to perfection. And He succeeds entirely in this through His Son, the God-man, Jesus. As a result, He is able to redeem all of mankind. All who accept His redemption.

Peter unveils to us the metaphor of the sinless, spotless Lamb:

> *For you know that God paid a ransom to save you from the empty life you inherited from your ancestors. And it was not paid with mere gold or silver, which lose their value. It was the precious blood of Christ, the sinless, spotless Lamb of God* (1 Peter 1:18-19).

As inferred above, the sinless, spotless quality of Jesus is what allowed Him to fulfill God's purpose. But the description of Him as the Lamb of God takes things a step further. Because the Israelites were required to offer sacrifice after sacrifice to atone for their sins, the depiction of Jesus as the Lamb is deeply revelatory, leading us to conclude that Jesus' sacrifice functions in the same manner as a typical animal sacrifice. All except one. The one where the Old Testament animal sacrifice does not destroy all sin for all time. *"For God's will was for us to be made holy by the sacrifice of the body of Jesus Christ, once for all time"* (Heb. 10:10).

> *Then I began to weep bitterly because no one was found worthy to open the scroll and read it. But one of the*

*twenty-four elders said to me, "Stop weeping! Look, the
Lion of the tribe of Judah, the heir to David's throne, has
won the victory. He is worthy to open the scroll and its
seven seals"* (Revelation 5:4-5).

Some imagine Jesus to be a tame little lamb, meek and mild. But
He is both. Meek and ferocious. Mild and terrible. He is the Lion
and the Lamb. He has won it all for His people. And He will not be
put up, shut up, or beat up. The next time He shows up, it will be as
a rider on a white horse, attaining the final victory for the whole of
the Kingdom of God.

Hebrews 7 reveals Jesus as High Priest forever.

While this topic is a little more complex, it is entirely understandable in the context of Jesus as the sinless, spotless Lamb.

*There were many priests under the old system, for death
prevented them from remaining in office. But because
Jesus lives forever, his priesthood lasts forever. Therefore
he is able, once and forever, to save those who come to God
through him. He lives forever to intercede with God on their
behalf. He is the kind of high priest we need because he is
holy and blameless, unstained by sin. He has been set apart
from sinners and has been given the highest place of honor
in heaven. Unlike those other high priests, he does not need
to offer sacrifices every day. They did this for their own
sins first and then for the sins of the people. But Jesus did
this once for all when he offered himself as the sacrifice for
the people's sins. The law appointed high priests who were
limited by human weakness. But after the law was given,
God appointed his Son with an oath, and his Son has been
made the perfect High Priest forever* (Hebrews 7:23-28).

Even the high priests assigned by God—the Levites—were incapable of truly standing in the gap for the people of God. But Jesus
stands as the one, true Advocate for God's people. (Incidentally, verse

25 also lends weight to the idea that the chief end of man is to come to God. Not to Jesus. *"Therefore he* [Jesus] *is able, once and forever, to save those **who come to God** through him.")* The high priest was always meant to serve as a facilitator. A connector of sorts. To reconcile God's people to Himself.

Imagining Jesus as a brother is something we don't often do. But Romans 8:29 and Hebrews 2:11 refer to Him this way. The value in understanding Jesus this way is that it further solidifies His role as distinctive from the Father. It's not a stretch. Jesus is the Son of God, and we are the children of God. Intriguingly, this makes us brothers with our Lord.

Speaking of Lord, I did have some trouble with wrapping my head around the idea of what it means for Jesus to be Lord in relation to God the Father.

Jesus as Savior is easy. We've covered that part sufficiently. But Jesus as Lord? If He is Lord, where does that leave God?

As you may have guessed, it's straightforward.

> *Therefore, God elevated him to the place of highest honor and gave him the name above all other names, that at the name of Jesus every knee should bow, in heaven and on earth and under the earth, and every tongue declare that Jesus Christ is Lord, to the glory of God the Father* (Philippians 2:9-11).

Did you see that? Just when I thought I might be spouting heresy, the Word of God affirmed this principle. Our key phrase is *to the glory of God the Father.* As Jesus fulfills His role as Lord and Savior, He does so, ultimately, for His Father's glory, not His own. So, Jesus is to be worshiped—as the name above every other name—above every other name, of course, except God the Father's.

AWAKENED TO THE HOLY SPIRIT

Ironically, many are desperately divided on the role of the Holy Spirit. Some ignorantly reject the work of the Spirit as something relegated to a few short years during the apostles' lifetime; while others hold Him as the primary person of God we're to build relationship with and, in doing so, neglect the Father and the Son.

I implore each reader to be guarded against these two extremes.

I grew up in a mainline evangelical church background, and we fell into the first camp. Maybe not quite to that extreme, but enough so that we were rarely taught about the person of the Spirit of God. Enough that I assumed anyone who prophesied or spoke in tongues was a total weirdo at best.

Guess that made Jesus and His disciples a bunch of oddballs, too.

In my ignorance, I missed so much.

I had little understanding of the pertinent power the Spirit imparts to Christ-followers to help us resist the enemy, reject temptation, and live for God (see Gal. 5:16-25).

I didn't know Jesus had plans to baptize every believer with the Holy Spirit and with fire as a separate and distinct event from salvation (see Acts 1:5; 19:1-7).

I didn't know what Paul knew. That if the Ephesian believers in Acts 19 were already filled with the Spirit upon receiving salvation, he would have simply said, "Brothers, though you haven't heard of Holy Spirit baptism before, know that upon accepting Jesus Christ as Lord and Savior, you have automatically received this baptism. Now simply believe. Nothing further is needed."

But he didn't say that. He clearly differentiated between the baptism of John (with water) and the baptism of Jesus (with the Holy Spirit and fire, Luke 3:16). And then he took intentional steps to remedy the situation by laying his hands on the Ephesians that they might be filled with the Spirit.

I didn't know this either. That the Spirit of God used to simply live *with* people in Old Testament days, but that Jesus would now make a way for Him to live *in* people in our day (see John 14:17).

I didn't put two and two together, that the Spirit of God had—in the old covenant—been set aside only for big-time spiritual leaders. Specifically, for the purpose of completing tasks assigned by God to special men. I wasn't aware that the new covenant changed all of this by giving *every* believer access to the wonderful baptism of God's Spirit (see Acts 2:38-39)!

I didn't understand the purpose of Holy Spirit baptism as it accomplishes at least three things—empowers direct connection with God for awakened intimate relationship (through prayer and worship), provides revelation and deeper understanding of God's Word (through Bible study), and affirms a new-creation new-norm where we can live continuously in the miraculous and in obedience.

I didn't understand any of this. But I simply cannot overstate how important Holy Spirit baptism is for a powerful, awakened relationship with God.

You may have been told that people who speak in tongues are demon possessed. Or you may have swung the pendulum to the other extreme, connecting "God encounters" to goose bumps, grand emotions, and glory clouds. But let me reiterate. We must not fall prey to these extremes.

Just as with Jesus, the Holy Spirit lives primarily for one thing concerning human beings—to reconcile us to the Father. To restore us to glorious fellowship with the Almighty.

Of course, Jesus reports that the Holy Spirit will continue to reveal the Son and say whatever the Son tells Him to say. John 16 reminds us that the Spirit will do at least four things—convict the world of its sin, convict the world of God's righteousness, convict the world of the judgement to come, and guide us into all truth. But what is that truth? The truth that Jesus has given His life for us? Yes. But to what end? To restore us to relationship with the Father. This is His chief aim. That we might worship and become one with the Father of all Creation. Just as He and Jesus are.

AWAKENED TO THE FATHER

The clarifications we make about the Father are often overlooked. However they are extremely important, because they help to stir up our hearts to worship the One who is wild about us.

The first one is simple. He is inviting us—each one—to come directly to Him—not through a mediator as in times past. But, directly to Him.

Israel once rejected God's invitation to meet with Him personally, to hear His voice for themselves, as recorded in Exodus 19:9-11 and 20:19. Subsequently, the Old Testament mediator-based system was born. This system—begun in Moses' day—required men who desired access to God to approach Him indirectly, through a few powerful, God-sanctioned men.

This was never God's desire though. He designed each of us for personal relationship with Him. Each man, each woman, and each child. Individually. For intimacy.

Thankfully, God did not give up on this beautiful idea. And Jesus brings it full circle in John 16:26-27: *"Then you will ask in my name. I'm not saying I will ask the Father on your behalf, for the Father himself loves you dearly because you love me and believe that I came from God."*

Woah. Say that out loud! "The Father loves me dearly." Say it again. "The Father loves me dearly." This is something we desperately need to hear over and over. Why? Because many of us have inaccurately attributed whatever love we might receive from God as love that could only emanate from Jesus. We see God as the angry one and Jesus as the loving one. God as the fiery one and Jesus as the peaceful one. But this is simply not true. Not only does this utterly oversimplify the person of God, but the case can easily be made that both Jesus and God embody each and every one of these attributes—anger, peace, fire, compassion, zeal, and love.

The point I emphasize here is that God is not off in heaven, intolerantly and dismissively bidding Jesus to "go down there and take care of those people." No! He loves us just as well! In fact, John 17:23 reminds us that God loves us just as much as He loves Jesus. That much!

Consider the picture Jesus paints of the Father in the story of the prodigal son. Here we have a father who watches day in and day out for his wayward son's return home. But this father—upon seeing his son off in the distance—doesn't simply wave from afar with arms crossed and a suspicious look on his face. No, this prestigious man actually pulls up his robe and goes running like a wild race horse toward his rebellious child.

When he meets him, he grabs him. He hugs and kisses him. He can't stop grinning. He even calls upon his entire household to stop everything and celebrate the return of his lost son with a party to end all parties—all to express the deepest of loves to a son returning home from the brink of death.

Amazing!

Even so, we must shake ourselves in order to keep from missing the unexpected depth of beauty lying below the surface. This story is not only about the prodigal son and the older brother. It's as much about the Father as it is about anyone. Plus, it provides a huge reveal for those who haven't understood. For those who continually see God as the mean, old, angry dude who wants to kill everybody.

Truth is, our God is crazy mad about us! Not only does He love us, but He likes us too. The devil would love to keep this truth under wraps. To keep us numb to the unfathomable reality that our heavenly Father—the One who breathed life into all things—longs to walk in intimate fellowship with each one of us.

Please understand. He is the One who had the big *leave heaven to go chase after and redeem my people* idea to begin with. And He— together with Jesus and the Holy Spirit—actually loves us deeply. Insanely. Completely.

Secondly, we must become joyfully aware that God has forever bridged the chasm between us by inviting us to pray directly to Him. With no middle man. Check this out. Jesus explains, *"At that time you won't need to ask me for anything. I tell you the truth, you will ask the Father directly, and he will grant your request because you use my name. You haven't done this before. Ask, using my name, and you will receive, and you will have abundant joy"* (John 16:23-24).

Now, don't freak. I'm not suggesting it is wrong to pray to Jesus. But in Jesus' own words, He clearly outlines the intended design while letting us know that this is somewhat of a new idea. To the people of that day. (Though it really shouldn't be a new idea to 21st century believers.)

I know, I know. We've been taught to pray to Jesus since we were knee high to a June bug. But, astonishingly, this is not what Jesus himself taught. Can you see how praying only to Jesus could subtly undermine the idea of increased fellowship with the Father? *Ironically, if we continually approach only Jesus in prayer, we are simultaneously eroding the idea that coming to the Father is the chief end in life.* Gratefully, Jesus corrects us gently by inviting us to pray more like this: "Dear Father, thank you for...." And to finish or transition like this: "...in Jesus' name I pray, amen."

Please, don't get weird about this. Just follow Jesus' instructions. I know. Human traditions die hard.

And let's promise not to make this a super religious sticking point. Praying to Jesus is not a sin. Praying to the Holy Spirit is not a sin. But *never* praying to God, our Father—the One who loves us dearly—is definitely odd. I mean, if Jesus says it, shouldn't we do it? Heaven forbid we refuse to follow Jesus' instructions in favor of our own traditions.

For posterity's sake, here's one more example of how Jesus instructs us to pray. You might recognize it. "Our Father, who art in heaven...."

With me?

Good.

Of course, Jesus is praying too. For all of us. As an intercessor. To whom? The Father. To what end? That we would become one with the Father, just as He is.

> I am praying not only for these disciples but also for all who will ever believe in me through their message. I pray that they will all be one, just as you and I are one—as you are in me, Father, and I am in you. And may they be in us so that the world will believe you sent me (John 17:20-21).

How does it work? How is it possible? Becoming one? I confess. I don't know exactly either. But I receive it and act upon it all in faith, nonetheless.

Want to be like Jesus? Here's your chance! Come to the Father. In worship. In relationship. In friendship. It's the most beautiful place, where all of God's children are joined together perfectly. With God, the Father. God, the Son. And God, the Spirit.

UNDER GOD'S AUTHORITY

Again, I want to make it absolutely clear that I am in no way suggesting that Jesus or the Holy Spirit are not to be worshiped or that they are somehow a lesser part of "God" than the Father is. That's ridiculous. And as I said earlier, I am not attempting to demote Jesus. Or the Holy Spirit, for that matter. I will confess, however, that we need to be very, very cautious not to elevate Jesus or the Holy Spirit above the Father, as some seem to do, either out of ignorance or as a result of deception.

> We need to be very, very cautious not to elevate Jesus or the Holy Spirit above the Father.

We get it. The name of Jesus is crazy powerful. Like no other name. No other name under God, that is. That's right. At Jesus' name, demons will tremble. At Jesus' name, sickness must die. At Jesus' name, darkness will flee. At Jesus' name, death, fear, shame, depression, disease, rage, and sin are all defeated! Hallelujah!

But is that the end? No. It's just the beginning. Vanquishing fear and death and hell and the grave is not the ending point. It's the starting point. These things were all standing in the way of one thing. That thing? Fellowship with God the Father. And they absolutely had to be eradicated by Jesus—not so we could relish in the fact that Jesus is bigger than all of the other heavenly beings—but so the path to relationship with the Father could be made clear. Once and for all. So all of the hurdles and pitfalls standing between us and communion with our First Love could finally be fully removed!

The Father Himself loves us dearly. And He has moved heaven and earth—in partnership with His Son and His Spirit—to reconcile us to Himself. Make no mistake. He will have His way. He will rule gloriously and beautifully with truth, love, and justice over all, establishing a beautiful portrait of all of creation living together in awakened, intimate fellowship with Him, under His good and perfect reign.

Picture this mind-blowing scene:

> *Just as everyone dies because we all belong to Adam, everyone who belongs to Christ will be given new life. But there is an order to this resurrection: Christ was raised as the first of the harvest; then all who belong to Christ will be raised when he comes back. After that the end will come, when he will turn the Kingdom over to God the Father, having destroyed every ruler and authority and power. For Christ must reign until he humbles all his enemies beneath his feet. And the last enemy to be destroyed is death. For the Scriptures say, "God has put all things under his authority." (Of course, when it says "all things are under his authority," that does not include God himself, who gave Christ his authority.) Then, when all things are under his authority, the Son will put himself under God's authority, so that*

God, who gave his Son authority over all things, will be utterly supreme over everything everywhere (1 Corinthians 15:22-28).

Enough said.

CHAPTER 14

AMERICAN IDOLATRY

*"Nothing teaches us about the preciousness
of the Creator as much as when we learn
the emptiness of everything else."*
—CHARLES SPURGEON

I'M GOING TO confess right up front that this chapter is going to burn like a fire. So, suit up and rock on.

In America, we typically don't bill ourselves as an idol-worshiping culture. Don't get me wrong. This is changing some. Unfortunately. But still, the majority of folks living in this nation—and in Western cultures in general—do not yet boast of having statues of wood or gold in their homes to worship.

Even so, as we look deeper into the question of *who* we should worship, it is often very helpful to pause and consider who we should *not* worship.

When I was in high school, I was a leader in my youth group, and I loved the Lord passionately. Occasionally, our youth pastor or some conference speaker would teach on idolatry. I listened intently and tried to process what it all meant.

It was difficult. Though I understood the whole "do not worship any other gods," thing, and the "do not make idols of any kind" thing, how did all this concern a nice kid living in Indianapolis, Indiana, going to Lawrence North High School, who loved God, read his Bible, and went to church a couple times a week? What could I possibly learn from all this? And how could I apply it to my life?

MORE THAN MEETS THE EYE

It wasn't like I was living some secret life where I gathered with friends to worship our ancestors or to hold séances. I wasn't hiding out in the basement collecting gold chains, crosses, and earrings from all the kids on my block with plans to melt them down in order to make a statue of a young calf. Nope. Nor did I wait until my parents went to sleep to pull out my miniature statue of Buddha from under my bed.

These things were completely foreign to me. And to the friends I knew. And to their friends. Even if many of these people didn't follow Jesus. We didn't worship other gods. We didn't worship cattle. We didn't bow to the sun or exalt the gods of Greek mythology. It was simple.

But wait.

What if there was more to it? I wondered. What if there was something I wasn't seeing? Something that had crept into our lives without us realizing it? Though we were not worshiping foreign gods directly, maybe we had adopted some of their customs. Their ideologies. Without noticing. Without harmful intent. What if we had begun thinking—and even acting—similarly to those who worshiped these foreign gods, all without calling them by name? And what if— by default—we were honoring them, worshiping them indirectly by adopting their errant truths for our lives?

Honestly, I've always been somewhat flippant toward the idea that I could ever fall prey to idol worship. Even subconsciously omitting the first and second laws from the Ten Commandments as part of my assumed immunity.

Still, I reflected. What did it mean to be an idol worshiper? Were we simply considering physical statues and handmade graven images, or was it something more? Something deeper? Could it be that idolatry was all around us? Instead of being something that was relegated to "those people" back in ancient Bible times or "those people" from third-world countries? What if idolatry was secretly seeping into every aspect of our lives? Even in these modern times?

What if idolatry involved things as simple as holding on to unbiblical standards? What if idolatry simply meant loving the things God hates? What if greed is idolatry? What if living for self is idolatry? What if idolatry is simply celebrating aspects of God's creation above God Himself?

PARADOXICAL JESUS

My dad told me a story once. He heard it from a missionary working with believers from a small local church in a developing nation. After spending a few days with these humble followers of Christ, he marveled at their joy and contentedness—especially in the face of poverty and seeming destituteness. He spoke honestly with the pastor. "I just don't know how you continue to walk so freely and passionately with the Lord when you are stricken with such poverty. Honestly, how do you maintain your joy and love for God when you have nothing!"

The pastor smiled and looked lovingly into the missionary's eyes. "Truthfully, my friend, I don't know how you make it in America when you have so much. There, you have no need for God. No need for a Savior. No need for provision. Here, all we have is Jesus."

Incredible.

The fact that we have so much in countries like America makes following Jesus harder, not easier. Unquestionably, having instant access to the greatest technology, up-to-the-minute information, and seemingly unending resources puts us on a much slipperier slope as we attempt to live a life of true holiness unto God—a life of complete dedication—void of the snares of idolatry.

Am I suggesting that less fortunate people are incapable of idolatry? No. But once an impoverished person has surrendered their life to Jesus, there isn't near the allurement to pull away from God. Why? Surely, in this instance, God is often much easier seen as Deliverer—as Provider—as Healer—as Savior—to those with little. We, Westerners, have too many other promising "saviors."

Think of the Parable of the Sower in Matthew 13:18-23. We hardly notice. But after sharing this story, we realize Jesus hits on this concept in verse 22: *"The seed that fell among the thorns represents those who hear God's word, but all too quickly the message is crowded out by the worries of this life and the lure of wealth, so no fruit is produced."*

Notice, it is the lure of wealth and the cares or worries of this life that often keep "seekers" from receiving the Word of the Lord. It was true back then, and it is true in our day.

Jesus emphasizes this all-too-real struggle again in Matthew 19.

> *Then Jesus said to his disciples, "I tell you the truth, it is very hard for a rich person to enter the Kingdom of Heaven. I'll say it again—it is easier for a camel to go through the eye of a needle than for a rich person to enter the Kingdom of God!" The disciples were astounded. "Then who in the world can be saved?" they asked. Jesus looked at them intently and said, "Humanly speaking, it is impossible. But with God everything is possible"* (Matthew 19:23-26).

Of course, it would be irresponsible to focus solely on the idolatry of the rich. God knows idolatry isn't prejudiced when it comes to economic background. Even so, this is sobering news for the wealthy, because many of our "poorest" in the West still live in luxury compared to much of the rest of the world. By God's grace, it is possible for all people—whether rich or poor—to enter the Kingdom of Heaven. Though it is clearly nothing short of a miracle for any of us.

BOTH GOD AND MOLECH

Zephaniah is a book that tends to collect a lot of dust, except possibly to quote—as I did earlier—Zephaniah 3:17. Still, it contains other compelling stories, like the passage in chapter one that brings us face to face with an element of idolatry that flies neatly under the radar. Here, God accuses the Israelites of worship of the false god, Molech. But not *only* of Molech. No. He decisively denounces them for worshiping both God *and* Molech—simultaneously. A deception we may be a little less familiar with.

Molech was originally one of the many false gods of the Ammonites that Israel was warned about. Molech was often associated with child sacrifice or at least referred to as a god who demanded radical allegiance.

Wait! Don't stop reading.

Here again, we may be tempted to roll our eyes and blow past this tired warning, disassociating ourselves from Molech because of our obvious connection with the one true God. You know, the One we dress up nice for on Sundays? The One we sing about in our National Anthem? The One whose name we use to amp up our curse words. Yeah. That One.

Ha. Not so fast. As implied, there is still one subtle yet critical matter we must consider. Zephaniah 1:5 makes it plain: *"For they go up to their roofs and bow down to the sun, moon, and stars. They claim to follow the Lord, but then they worship Molech, too."*

What?

Don't miss it. The irony is, of course, found in that last little three-letter word.

The New King James Version puts it this way: *"Those who worship the host of heaven on the housetops; those who worship and swear oaths by the Lord, but who also swear by Milcom."* (Milcom is another name for Molech.)

When I read this the first time, my heart skipped a beat.

Have you ever known something before you knew it? That's how I felt.

Could it be? That we might be worshiping the one true God "with all of our heart"—*and*, at the same time, worshiping other gods "with all of our soul"? As revealed by our choices, our false beliefs, and our not-so-obvious sinful habits? Yikes. I hadn't thought of it quite like that before. I figured it was one or the other. Either a worshiper of God or a worshiper of false gods. (Hopefully the former.) But, I never considered it could be *both*.

Frighteningly, this passage reveals a not-so-scenic scenic view where we are introduced to the idea that we may be worshiping both the one true God and a few false gods. Without realizing it. Both God *and* gods. Both God *and* man. Both God *and* His creation. Both God *and* false ideologies. Which, of course, is not okay.

If this isn't enough, Zephaniah continues.

> *Stand in silence in the presence of the Sovereign Lord, for the awesome day of the Lord's judgment is near. The Lord has prepared his people for a great slaughter and has chosen their executioners. "On that day of judgment," says the Lord, "I will punish the leaders and princes of Judah and all those following pagan customs. Yes, I will punish those who participate in pagan worship ceremonies, and those who fill their masters' houses with violence and deceit"* (Zephaniah 1:7-9).

Okay, Jeff. Now, you've taken things a bit too far. This book is starting to feel preachy. Judgmental. You know? I mean, do we *really* participate in pagan worship ceremonies—right here in good ol' America the beautiful?

Good question.

IN SEARCH OF AN EARTHLY GOD

When it comes to the issue of modern-day idolatry, I've heard it said there are two types of people. Those searching for a "star" to idolize—talented actors, artists, entrepreneurs, athletes, etc.—and those dreaming of becoming said "stars." Either way, the issue is the same. It's a risky game.

Of course, no chapter entitled "American Idolatry" is complete without at least one reference to our favorite reality TV shows like *American Idol, The Voice, America's Got Talent,* and *The X Factor.*

These shows have been wildly successful. Obviously.

Whether or not you are a fan, it's clear to us all—as many a producer knows—that audiences worldwide clamor for episode after episode.

But, have you ever really asked yourself why?

I find it interesting that we crave this type of entertainment. Over others. Maybe it's our passion for the underdog—our simple sympathy for those big dreamer types who desperately desire a destiny of serenading the masses. Or maybe it's just our wild love for music and our insatiable appetite for discovering God's newly found creatives.

Maybe.

Or maybe it's more than that. I mean, the show *is* called *American Idol* for a reason.

Go figure.

Ponder this. What is the bottom line for these shows? Isn't it to scour the planet—searching under every rock, in every dark corner, in every nook, and in every cranny—for someone who can be fashioned into a bright light? Someone we can all gather around and goggle at? Someone who will blow our minds and lead us nearer to a state of euphoria, as we stand, cheer, and shout—literally teary-eyed—in awe of our newfound troubadour?

Come on, Jeff. Don't you know it's just about the money? The power? Yes. Of course. But it's not about money and power for the millions of viewers.

It's about that feeling we get. The one that rises inside when that unassuming someone steps up to the microphone, stares nervously at the floor and then at the cameras, stutters and stammers through a few introductory questions, and then opens their mouth to sing to the utter amazement of our senses. Oh, those mellifluous vocal tones!

I get it. I've scrolled through the YouTube videos too!

But shouldn't we be asking ourselves. What's the hidden agenda? Too cynical? Maybe.

Maybe not.

Along with a bit of fun on a Monday evening, there are plenty of mixed motives—some good and some, well, not-so-good. If we're honest, we can clearly see that there is a deep longing inside well-meaning people everywhere to unearth something beyond ourselves—something to glory in—someone to be amazed by.

It's like in the 2004 animated smash hit movie *The Incredibles*. The little tyke on the trike stares longingly at Mr. Incredible after being asked, "Well, what are *you* waiting for?" and then sheepishly responds, "I don't know. Something amazing, I guess?" Which, of course, leads Mr. Incredible to mutter, "Me too, kid. Me too."

It's the ultimate human quest. The mission of missions. The hunt for something amazing. For the thing we all long for. For the one piece that could bring the entire puzzle together. Something profound. Something captivating. Something beyond our imagination. Something, or someone, ultimately, worthy of our worship.

It definitely exposes that thing raging deep inside us—placed there by God Himself—that yearns to worship. That longs to be amazed. And yet—like the Israelites—we remain wearied with the obvious answer. We search and search—willing to climb every monstrous mountain, cross every dastardly desert, and swim every storming sea. If only to find "it." Yet, when all the roads to "it" lead straight back to our Creator, we are still driven—whether in defiance or ignorance or pride—to turn away and fashion our very own ready-made god. All the while, the one true God is there in plain view. Do we acknowledge Him? No. We ignore Him and refuse to worship Him, pulling close to our chest even the very things He has created—whether wood, gold, or human. Whether talent, riches, or power. My very own glorious idol. My precious.

FANTASTIC FROZEN FOOTBALL FRENZY

The often-awkward metaphors of prostitution and adultery are used regularly in the Bible. From Jeremiah to Hosea, these themes are all too common. While God has dubbed us His bride and announced Himself as our groom, He is continually forsaken for our many lovers.

Lovers? Yes. All the other "mistresses" that steal our hearts and rob us of a first-love love for the Father.

I couldn't help but laugh—and cry—at a recent Instagram post by a friend. It was an actual photo of the December 10, 2017 week-14 NFL game featuring the Buffalo Bills and the Indianapolis Colts in a match for the ages. What made it so outstanding? Well, it was near white-out conditions with up to sixteen inches of fresh falling snow on the field throughout the entire game. Try as they might to clear the lines on the field, the snow was just too dominant a force.

We saw an extra missed field goal or two, plenty of end zone snow-angel celebrations, and way too many "face fulls" of the powdery white stuff there in the Buffalo Bills' Ralph Wilson Stadium.

You might have thought the Bills fans would have sat this one out. But the near capacity crowd remained—in blankets and in heavy coats—for the entirety of the game, which concluded with a spectacular touchdown gallop from LeSean McCoy, icing the game at 13-7 and sending the Colts back to the locker room with visions of thawing out sometime next spring.

The photo my pastor friend posted was of the crowd—seated on ice-hardened seats and covered with new snow. The caption read: "Well pastor, I don't come to church because I don't like sitting that long and the seats aren't very comfortable."

For good measure, he included an emoji with tears of joy.

Stupendous!

Of course, you knew we couldn't talk about worship without bringing up football, right? It's the ultimate example we Christian leaders turn to. I mean, what better way to make people feel guilty than by messing with their sports?

Nevertheless, I wonder. How is it we can jump up and down, do cartwheels, and scream at the top of our lungs at a bunch of guys running around chasing an odd-shaped ball, and yet act so humdrum when it comes to God. It just don't make sense!

If you know me, I love football. I'll be the first one to holler and shout and bounce off the walls when the Denver Broncos pull out a close one—much like I did when the Vikings pulled off the Minneapolis Miracle against the New Orleans Saints on Sunday night, January 14, 2018.

> One day we will see clearly the utter fools we have been in idolizing and consuming the things of this world while ignoring or patronizing the One who gave us all we have.

With ten seconds on the clock and no timeouts, and the end zone 61 yards away, Minnesota's Case Keenum (who is now a Bronco) stepped up to take the snap with little hope of overcoming the one-point deficit created by a last-second Saints field goal. Rooting for the Vikings because of the Broncos losing season, I felt that lump in my throat. It was inevitable. The game was over. This play was merely a formality. A finality.

But wait.

Magically, Keenum stepped back to throw, and somehow his rainbow of a pass floated effortlessly to Stefon Diggs. Diggs leaped through the air and grabbed the long bomb, all while avoiding the obvious approaching tackler. Maintaining his balance with a single hand on the ground, he spun around and scrambled like a shooting star into the end zone, reawakening the stunned home crowd to victorious pandemonium. As the clock struck zero.

I joined right in! My whole family did. We were screaming, hooting, and hollering, grabbing each other, and holding our heads in our hands in utter amazement. Just like everyone in that stadium. (Except for the Saints.)

We couldn't believe it.

The announcer yelled out spontaneously, "It's a Minneapolis Miracle!"

We agreed!

Wow, what fun.

Thing is—and we do have to ask—just why is it that we can cheer uncontrollably for man, and yet refuse to cheer even half as much for God? The One who formed us from the dust. The One who set us free from death, hell, and the grave? Isn't it obvious that something is amiss?

Maybe it's because God never pulled off a stunt quite like Case Keenum.

Really? Um, no.

You know, the whole Jesus on the cross thing? Where it looked like He was toast, and then—just when everybody had that horrible lump in their throat like the game was over and the devil had shocked the heavens—He showed up all divine and stuff, alive again, just as the clock struck zero?

Yeah. That stunt.

(Incidentally, just to be clear, I am not attempting to equate the Saints to the devil. Just saying.)

Look. Nobody takes issue with the guy who endures and enjoys the three-hour, snow-blitzed Buffalo game. I certainly don't. That is, unless that same guy refuses to go to the same lengths for his Creator. His Savior. Unless that same guy moans about a 15-minute prayer meeting or rolls his eyes at the preacher's call to holiness. Unless that same guy can't muster the stamina to remain standing for

more than four and a half minutes during the musical worship portion of the service.

Of course, we're not referring to unbelievers. We're talking
about churchgoers.

It's pure insanity. Honestly. That we would—that we could—be
so insanely passionate about the things of earth—that ultimately mean
nothing—while remaining so lackluster toward the things of heaven.

I'm convinced. One day—either at the second coming or otherwise—our eyes will be supernaturally opened, and we will see
clearly—likely for the first time—the utter fools we have been in
idolizing and consuming the things of this world while ignoring or
patronizing the One who gave us all we have.

ONE NIGHT STAND

Take a long look at this sobering Scripture passage from Jeremiah 2.
Or ponder the last few pages and come back to this.

> "You say, 'That's not true!
> I haven't worshiped the images of Baal!'
> But how can you say that?
> Go and look in any valley in the land!
> Face the awful sins you have done.
> You are like a restless female camel
> desperately searching for a mate.
> You are like a wild donkey,
> sniffing the wind at mating time.
> Who can restrain her lust?
> Those who desire her don't need to search,
> for she goes running to them!
> When will you stop running?
> When will you stop panting after other gods?
> But you say, 'Save your breath.

I'm in love with these foreign gods,
and I can't stop loving them now!'
Israel is like a thief
who feels shame only when he gets caught.
They, their kings, officials, priests, and prophets—
all are alike in this.
To an image carved from a piece of wood they say,
'You are my father.'
To an idol chiseled from a block of stone they say,
'You are my mother.'
They turn their backs on me,
but in times of trouble they cry out to me,
'Come and save us!'
But why not call on these gods you have made?
When trouble comes, let them save you if they can!
For you have as many gods
as there are towns in Judah.
Why do you accuse me of doing wrong?
You are the ones who have rebelled,"
says the Lord.
"I have punished your children,
but they did not respond to my discipline.
You yourselves have killed your prophets
as a lion kills its prey.
O my people, listen to the words of the Lord!
Have I been like a desert to Israel?
Have I been to them a land of darkness?
Why then do my people say, 'At last we are free from God!
We don't need him anymore!'
Does a young woman forget her jewelry,

or a bride her wedding dress?
Yet for years on end
my people have forgotten me.
How you plot and scheme to win your lovers.
Even an experienced prostitute could learn from you!"
(Jeremiah 2:23-33)

Oh, my. You may want to read all that again. Maybe not. Maybe it's too much. Too illuminating. Too long.

But God does not mince words here. I really love Him for this. I'm eternally grateful He doesn't give us the ol' Minnesota-nice, passive-aggressive treatment. He is as real as it gets. In your face.

This passage gives us a description of a people who are chasing evil. They aren't just stumbling upon it. They're sniffing it out with a vengeance. Yet they don't see it. Yet they do, because they crave it. They want it. They need it.

In many ways, we don't notice our adultery. We don't notice the way we use God for a quick fix. In the same way a person would look casually to a prostitute for one night of pleasure. Or even the way two strangers might casually jump in the sack for the thrill of it. We too run to church—to God—for the feel-goods. Sometimes. For the goose bumps. Or even to make ourselves feel better concerning our spiritual obligations.

Let's be honest. Instead of reading our Bible with hopes of receiving true revelation from God's heart, we read it to check off our list—to feel a little better about the bad choices we're making.

Instead of praying with a longing for fellowship with the Father, we pray as a political statement—as a way to show others our spiritual aptitude.

At the same time, we don't notice how we prostitute—yes, prostitute—ourselves, clambering for one lover after another after another.

Help us, Lord.

Take technology. Seriously? Yes. Can we say addiction? And still, we sincerely believe that buying the hottest phone or gadget is as important as breathing.

Isn't this worship?

Take food. Yep! I know this is a sensitive subject. But when are we going to stop shoving absurd quantities of processed foods into our pie hole, which in turn is now forcing us to shove absurd quantities of dangerous meds into our pie hole as a remedy?

Isn't this worship?

Take sex. Can we be real? It's bad. We're in a mess with this one. And sadly, I don't even know how to write about it without sounding cliché. We're just too numb. It's just become too normal. There's the obvious. The billion-dollar porn industry. Yes, *billion*. But let's forget about that for a minute. The easy access for our sons and daughters to soft porn in PG-13 and R rated movies and TV shows is insane. But, whatever. What are we to do? Oh well. We'll just invite it all right into our homes through our many screens.

The sick things we would never allow to walk through our front door—we now allow right in our living room. Tucked neatly behind a screen. For innocent—not-so-innocent—little eyes to see. Is it any different? And we gobble it all up in mass quantity.

Isn't this worship?

Take time. How can we say we don't have time for God? We make time for everything else. *Everything* else. Seriously, He's the one who created time in the first place. And yet, sadly, we believe it's just the way it has to be. Rushing. Pressure. Competition. Mortgage. Providing the "better life" for the kids. It's one rationalization after another.

Isn't this worship?

And yet, our gracious heavenly Father still has mercy. Still, He replies in Jeremiah 3:

> *Therefore, go and give this message to Israel. This is what the Lord says:*

"O Israel, my faithless people,
come home to me again,
for I am merciful.
I will not be angry with you forever.
Only acknowledge your guilt.
Admit that you rebelled against the Lord your God
and committed adultery against him
by worshiping idols under every green tree.
Confess that you refused to listen to my voice.
I, the Lord, have spoken!
Return home, you wayward children,"
says the Lord,
"for I am your master.
I will bring you back to the land of Israel—
one from this town and two from that family—
from wherever you are scattered.
And I will give you shepherds after my own heart,
who will guide you with knowledge and understanding"
(Jeremiah 3:12-15).

Grace. Mercy. Compassion.

Amazing.

But will we?

Acknowledge our guilt?

Confess our rebellion?

Return home?

Good question.

Maybe we're just like the smoker who says, "I can quit any time I want to."

Know what's scary? Idolatry is sneakier than many of the other obvious worldly temptations. It shows up unannounced. Unopposed.

Because we underestimate it. We could be one of the thousands who goes to church every week (or more likely two to three times a month, based on national averages) who unknowingly engages relationally with everything on God's green earth. Everything. Except God.

It's time to wake up. It's time we were challenged. Challenged to acknowledge our guilt, confess our rebellion, and return home.

Maybe this has struck a chord—maybe you've begun to realize you've missed it in the *who* category of worship. Take this opportunity to make it right. Right now. Or, if you're not sure, simply ask your Father to reveal to you the ways you may be unintentionally worshiping idols.

Then repent. Receive the cleansing blood of Jesus. Be made new in the power of the Holy Spirit. And be awakened to the unadulterated worship of your Father in heaven. Then go, and "idolatry" no more.

CHAPTER 15

KING AND FRIEND

*"And they began to think up foolish
ideas of what God was like."*
—THE APOSTLE PAUL

AS YOU MIGHT have guessed, how we worship God is typically tied
to who God is to us. Like it or not, we each tend to approach Him the
way we understand Him best. In association with our circumstances,
our upbringing, our culture, our grid.

For this reason, I can't help but wonder if we're missing out on
all of His fullness as a result—thus keeping ourselves from enjoying certain aspects of His nature that don't resonate with ours yet are
essential to a deepening, authentic relationship with Him.

Of course, the beauty here is that God can and should be
approached in a variety of ways. Yet the danger is compounded when
we focus on only one or two aspects of His divine nature while overlooking or avoiding others. As a result, we inevitably manufacture our
very own false god in the process. And we're right back to Chapter 14.

Seems like we're searching. Searching for a god we can more
easily relate to—one that fits more neatly into our own little world,
instead of the One true, glorious God who defies containment, all
while holding the world—and you and I—in His hands.

THE PENDULUM

Take this question. Is God to be worshiped as Consuming Fire or Abba Father? Most of us are aware that God is referred to by Paul as a consuming fire in Hebrews 12:29, and yet we also recognize that God reveals Himself as "Abba Father"—Aramaic for Daddy—in Romans 8:15. But no matter how we try, still, we tend to prefer one or the other—influenced greatly by our personalities and our own limited understanding of His character—especially when it comes to relating to Him through prayer and worship.

This is dangerous.

Even so, it seems with every passing generation the pendulum swings back and forth with trends rather than with truths that guide our approach to worshiping God. The fog tends to thicken with each century gone by. Three to four hundred years ago, worship was full of solemn chants and seemingly lifeless liturgy. The reason? Because, as anticipated, people worship God in the way they define Him—in this case, as a far-away, foreboding, overbearing dictator. Today, however, we've nearly flipped the script with musical worship that can often be characterized as familiar, casual, or popular. Why? Because of the way we've grown accustomed to seeing God in these times.

> It seems with every passing generation the pendulum swings back and forth with trends rather than truths that guide our approach to worshiping God.

As a man-pleasing, hyper-loving, grace-abusing Santa Claus pushover.

Too harsh?

Think about it.

I know it's harder to identify the deception in the latter of the two descriptions above. Seriously. How could this "modern" assessment of God actually impede our approach to Him? Isn't God a good Father who loves giving good gifts to His children? Isn't He slow to anger and full of unfailing love? Isn't He quick to extend mercy and grace, answering those who call on His name?

Of course.

But He is also a good Father who calls us to suffering and trials (see 1 Pet. 1:6-7; 2:21; 4:12-14). A good Father who disciplines His children (see Heb. 12:10-11; 12:5-9). And a good Father who is both Defender and Judge (see John 5:22; 2 Cor. 5:10; James 5:9).

Can you see how easily we overlook foundational, balancing aspects of God's character? Even as we attempt to avoid slicing Him up any which way we please, we must also recognize how devoted the enemy is to pushing us to one extreme or the other. Why? Because he knows full well when we disregard *some* of who God is, we are only a few steps away from disregarding *all* of who He is.

He's not stupid. (Clearly.) He understands better than we can possibly imagine how closely our view of Him is tied to our approach to worshiping Him. And just how seriously this decreases our ability to cultivate an accurate, authentic relationship with Him.

It's the same with humans. Significant unknowns typically hinder the development of heathy, fully transparent relationships, just as the lack of understanding for God's revealed character grossly limits—and even prevents entirely—the possibility of real friendship with Him.

Sound daunting? Take comfort, my friend. Jeremiah reminds, *"In those days when you pray, I will listen. If you look for me wholeheartedly, you will find me"* (Jer. 29:12-13).

This is great news. He *will* listen. And we *will* find Him! The only question is, are we looking? Are we searching? Clearly, Jeremiah isn't advocating the idea that we will find Him regardless of our approach. No. He encourages us to understand that we will find Him only *if* we are looking for Him. But not simply *if* we are looking for Him, but *if* we are looking for Him with our whole heart. Then He will be revealed to us.

Revealed. Yes, revealed.

Revealed means to make something known by divine or supernatural means.

The irony? Just as it is possible to find Him, it is also possible to miss Him. Without knowing it.

POLITICALLY INCORRECT JESUS

How else might we misunderstand God and thus be kept from worshiping Him as He is? As He desires?

As mentioned earlier—Jesus is the visible image of our invisible God. And this means our understanding of God the Father is entirely married to the scriptural revelation we've acquired concerning the Son. (Remember, the point of reading the Scriptures is not to know the Scriptures but to know the God of the Scriptures.)

For better or worse, we all see Jesus through a lens. One of pain, one of privilege, one of insecurity, or something else. The type of lens we're looking through determines the Jesus—and the God—we see. Many of us see Jesus inaccurately and, therefore, see God inaccurately. Maybe it's because—refusing to study for ourselves—we're only aware of what our pastor has said about Jesus. Maybe it's because—when push comes to shove—we don't really want to see Him as He is. Or maybe it's because of the blinders we wear—those of man-based religion, depression, or fear—that grossly cloud our vision.

It's for this reason that I decided to do something informative. As a result of the many inaccurate statements I often hear concerning Jesus, I decided to read through the Gospels, highlighting anything Jesus said or did that seemed to fly in the face of our modern-day, smaller-than-life portrayal of Jesus. Because we all—myself included—entertain preconceived notions of Jesus, I wanted to rediscover the bigger picture. From Scripture.

I highlighted things like:

- Matthew 8:22, where Jesus rebukes a prospective disciple by refusing to allow him to attend the burial of his own father in favor of following Him immediately.

- Matthew 8:26, where Jesus scolds His closest disciples for being fearful in a life-threatening storm: *"Why are you afraid? You have so little faith!"*

- Matthew 9:13, where Jesus offends the religious leaders by publically belittling their knowledge of the Bible, saying, "Go and learn the meaning of Hosea 6:6."

- Matthew 10:13, where Jesus encourages His followers to "take back the blessing" of anyone whose home is unworthy, as they would go from house to house sharing the Gospel.

- Matthew 10:34, where Jesus reminds the crowds that He didn't come to bring peace, but to bring a sword, turning one person against another.

- Matthew 11:16, where Jesus publically describes this generation as a group of whining and complaining children.

- Matthew 11:20, where Jesus denounces the cities where He did most of His miracles because they still refused to turn from their sins to God.

- Matthew 15:26, where Jesus calls the Gentile woman a dog right to her face and initially refuses to heal her daughter.

- Matthew 16:23, where Jesus turns to His friend, Peter, shouting, *"Get away from me, Satan! You are a dangerous trap to me!"*

- Matthew 17:17, where Jesus severely reprimands His own disciples: *"You faithless and corrupt people! How long must I be with you? How long must I put up with you?"*

And the list goes on and on, and on and on.

It's a list you won't see echoed in any of the best-selling leadership books. Yet Jesus knows a thing or two about leadership.

Why do I bring this list before you? To ridicule our Savior? No. To get you thinking. To bring you into the conversation. To provoke you in regards to whether you truly worship the Jesus of the Bible or simply the one you've created in your own mind. Because who Jesus is to you is paramount to how you worship.

BOTH AND

Of course, we could easily produce an equally impressive list of merciful and loving passages describing Jesus. The point of listing out the more intense passages is not to point out an overly harsh or abrasive Jesus, but to remind us of what the New Testament scripture in Romans 11:22 tells us; that *"God is both kind and severe."* Both and.

Could it be that our propensity to settle for one extreme over the other keeps us from knowing the One and only true God—the One who is Friend, King, Daddy, and Father? Lover and Lord? All of the above?

Isn't He the expressive, outspoken friend *and* the sit-in-a-room-quietly-without-words friend, too? Isn't He the God who speaks with a "still small voice" *and* the One who raises His voice to reprimand Saul on the road to Damascus? Isn't He brokenhearted over His lost children *and* filled with joy over His adopted sons and daughters? In all His facets, He is unequivocally calling us to be like Him. And to worship Him based on who *He* is, not on who *we* are.

What if we worship God only as Consuming Fire? Or as the faraway God so many imagine? Won't we be more prone to miss out on the intimate love and friendship He longs to impart to us as Daddy? What if we worship God only as intimate lover? Or simply as buddy or pal? Don't we risk overlooking His absolute authority and then potentially disregard Him as Sovereign Lord?

The beauty of God's nature is that He is not simply one thing or the other. God is every good thing. He is Groom, Coach, and Judge. He is Friend, Teacher, and Ruler. He is Brother, Counselor, and General. He is to be feared and to be loved. To be embraced intimately and to be reverenced absolutely. He is God. And when we come to Him as He is—in the fullness of all biblical revelation—we will find ourselves communing with a God who is like no other and who loves and cares for us like no other.

SECTION 4

HOW DO WE DO THIS WORSHIP THING?

CHAPTER 16

WITH HEART, SOUL, MIND, AND STRENGTH

"We should know and celebrate
God with our whole person."
—CRAIG S. KEENER

SOME COME SINGING. Some come dancing.

Some come quiet. Some come fearful.

Some come reverent. Some come reckless.

Some come joyful. Some come tearful.

It's true. Some folks worship like they're in a funeral home while others worship like they're in a dance club. Which is best? Does it matter? Do we care?

As discussed in the previous chapter, our view of *who* God is—as determined by our own revealed knowledge of the Scriptures—desperately influences *how* we worship Him. For better or worse.

This is where we get uber-practical by zeroing in on a few of the foremost activities and behaviors of bona fide God-worshipers—as inspired by God's Word. How do they act? How do they live? What traits best characterize them? What concrete changes can we begin to make in order to join these ordinary extraordinaries on our journey to awakening pure worship?

So glad you asked.

Psalm 2:11 stresses, *"Serve the Lord with reverent fear, and rejoice with trembling."* Here, we are reminded that *both* reverence and rejoicing are essential—though they are seemingly striking opposites. We note that *both* are expected and desired if we are to worship God in the manner He designed. The manner that is fitting—for us and for Him.

But how exactly does one approach the Creator with trembling *and* with rejoicing? Simultaneously? Try it. It ain't natural, y'all. And yet, it's in the mystery of this command that we discover the healthiest and most effective expression of awakened worship. The one that not only contributes best to the Kingdom but also to us personally, as it propels us purposefully like relational little satellites into perfect orbit around the Father, Son, and Holy Spirit.

I began noticing this *both and* principle woven throughout portions of Scripture years ago. It was present in Paul's call to pray and sing in the spirit *and* in the understanding (see 1 Cor. 14:15). It was documented in James' portrayal of salvation as it springs forth through faith *and* works (see James 2:17). And it was revealed poignantly again as Jesus exhorts us to worship the Father in spirit *and* in truth (see John 4:23). To list a few.

It stands to reason, then, that if we are being encouraged to recognize God's character from a *both and* perspective we must also purpose to respond to Him with a *both and* expression.

Amazingly, entire denominations are divided around the "in spirit and in truth" concept. Some folks are determined to approach God predominantly via knowledge and information—from more of a cerebral vantage point—while others are resolved to approach Him with a weighty emphasis on the experiential—from more of an emotional vantage point.

While both of these approaches stem from biblical teaching, each is fruitless apart from the other. *For if we imagine we have truth but are without spirit, the result is dead religion. Likewise, if we imagine we have spirit but are without truth, the result is empty emotion.* Both are utterly lifeless apart from the other, yet both are abundantly life-giving when intermingled.

ALL OF THE ABOVE

Most of my students at North Central University love multiple choice exams. At least this way, all of the possible answers are right there in front of them. Admittedly, it becomes a bit slipperier when the professor adds options like "both A and B" or "all of the above." But I guess that's the idea.

It reminds me of a list Jesus lays out in Mark 12:28, when He is quizzed on which commandment is the greatest by another teacher—a teacher of religious law. Jesus responds with this well-known assertion: *"And you must love the Lord your God with all your heart, all your soul, all your mind, and all your strength"* (Mark 12:30).

What we may not see huddled neatly between the lines is a God-given, foundational approach for *how* we should worship. An invitation of sorts. A blueprint for cultivating effectual relationship with a supernatural God. Something that should be impossible. Something that should be unthinkable. Something that is, quite honestly, entirely irrational.

Even so, Jesus makes the impossible possible as He frames His blueprint—in a sense—by laying out an unspoken awakening worship exam question:

Which of the following is the most effective way to love God?

A. With all your heart

B. With all your soul

C. With all your mind

D. With all your strength

E. A and D

F. B and C

G. All of the above

Admittedly, this is a tad elementary, yet I've noticed we often naively pick and choose our answers to Jesus' rhetorical questions based on what seems best suited to our personalities. Just as we often cherry-pick the attributes of God we identify with, leaving the less desirable ones on the table. We clearly use the same approach when it comes to the manner in which we express ourselves to God.

Those who know me well, know I'm a tad obsessed with teaching on the importance of balance in worship. They know I'm constantly challenging each of us to step out of our comfort zone to worship God always from a biblical point of view. Yet try as I might, people inevitably approach me after hearing me speak, saying, "You know, Jeff, I'm just not really the hand-raising type. I prefer to worship God from my heart." To which I playfully respond, "That's great. You're a fourth of the way there! Keep at it!"

After intentionally leaving an awkward silence—where they gaze at me perplexed—I rattle off a paraphrase of Mark 12:30 and clarify that worshiping God with all of our heart is remarkable but, of course, is not the whole enchilada.

Understandably, it's much easier to circle letter A than to stretch ourselves by embracing the response Jesus is leading us to, which is, of course, G. Why? Well, it could be ignorance. Or rebellion.

Rebellion?

Really?

Sure.

Each of us resists the things we are uncomfortable with. So, naturally, when we're uncomfortable with the *all of our mind* aspect of worshiping God, we avoid or simply ignore letter C altogether—as if it doesn't apply. Similarly, when we are uncomfortable with the *all of our strength* (or physical) expressions of worship—like lifting our hands, dancing, or kneeling—we tend to omit letter D, as well. Surprisingly, there are some folks who identify more closely with the physical expression of worship and who—as a result—fail to acknowledge the importance of engaging their heart, thereby sidestepping letter A.

All the while, God has done everything in His power to help us get beyond ourselves and realize the truth—that we are each designed, as awakened worshipers, to live out letter G—all of the above. Regardless of our natural bent. And to realize—as restrictive as it may sound—that there is truly no other answer.

Truth be told. *To love God with one or two of these approaches alone is tantamount to not loving God at all.* Don't be deceived. It may seem pleasant enough to come to God with *all of our mind*, but this merely compartmentalizes our love and leaves us grossly missing the mark. Loving God with *all of our soul* or *all of our heart* is just not the same as loving Him with our whole person. Heart, soul, mind, and strength. They're all connected, and they're all required for awakened worship.

A TIME FOR EVERYTHING

It has become clearer and clearer to me that each one of us is on a journey that requires adjustment—either slight or severe—in our approach to worshiping God. Much like every other area in our lives. I realize this can be terribly worrisome for some, but ask yourself, how much more worrisome is it for us to resist God's instructions rather than trust that He knows best? That there are incredible blessings and rewards—not to mention, greater fullness of life—in following God's guidelines.

Instead of making up our own ideas of who God is and how we should worship Him, what if we determined to approach this incredible supernatural Being via the full revelation of His Word. Crazy, right? I'm just saying. What do we have to lose? Ourselves, of course. But isn't that the point? If we did, we might just find ourselves worshiping God fittingly, purposefully—with rejoicing, trembling, intimacy, and reverence, enthusiasm, silence, celebration, and mourning. All of the above.

Ecclesiastes 3:1-8 helps.

A Time for Everything

For everything there is a season,
a time for every activity under heaven.
A time to be born and a time to die.
A time to plant and a time to harvest.
A time to kill and a time to heal.
A time to tear down and a time to build up.
A time to cry and a time to laugh.
A time to grieve and a time to dance.
A time to scatter stones and a time to gather stones.
A time to embrace and a time to turn away.
A time to search and a time to quit searching.
A time to keep and a time to throw away.
A time to tear and a time to mend.
A time to be quiet and a time to speak.
A time to love and a time to hate.
A time for war and a time for peace.

If you're like me, you find yourself inspired by some of these words yet repelled by others. I tend to resonate with words like *heal* and *embrace* and *speak up* more than with words like *war* and *tear* and *quiet*. Yet, Solomon reminds us that each of these applies at certain times.

There is a time to dance and a time to be still. In awakened worship. There is a time to cry and a time to laugh. In awakened worship. There is a time for peace and a time for war. In awakened worship. There is a time to be loud and a time to be silent. In awakened worship. As always, our *how* worship response is tied to our *who* God understanding.

I'm not saying God demands we all come to Him with exactly the same expression, all the time—robot-like—erasing the beauty of diversity in our personalities and expressions. No. He made us each unique. And still, we must avoid expressing ourselves to God exclusively according to our personalities, according to our incomplete and biased understanding of who He is. Why? Because He calls us daringly beyond our natural selves and into our supernatural selves—out of our world and into His.

> We must avoid expressing ourselves to God exclusively according to our personalities.

Let me explain.

FROM NATURAL TO SUPERNATURAL

As you might expect, it is not within my born nature to pick up and carry my cross. Likewise, it is not within yours to love your enemies. Nor are we naturally inclined to die to self. Yet, we are still expected to practice these Kingdom concepts, whether they jive with our natural personalities or not. As expected, our natural bent has no bearing on our supernatural responsibility to walk out God's commands.

Awakened worship expression is no different. Crammed full of helpful instructions, the Scriptures escort us boldly toward worshipful practices that are meant to enlarge—even transform—our lives.

Some make excuses. "Yeah, but I'm not really the expressive, shouting, or dancing kind of worshiper." Sure, I get it. I'm not the giving kind of person either. Yet I'm still asked to give. I'm not the humble kind of person either. Yet I'm still required to cast off my pride.

Imagine if, just prior to Joshua leading the Israelites in the infamous shout that brought down the walls of Jericho, one unassuming character raises his hand and says, "Oh, um, Josh? I'm just not really the shouting kind of person. I'm gonna need to sit this one out."

Hmmm, yeah. Not gonna happen.

Cue the lightning.

Of course, we can't bow out. Or drop out. We must all shout out! Every voice counts. Everybody yells. At the top of their lungs. All together. All by faith.

Does any of it make sense?

No. And yes.

You see, there are incredible benefits for us when we do as God commands. In life and in worship. Not just because we obey. But because the requirements God gives us are designed with our good in mind. When He asks us to shout, it's for our good! When He asks us to step beyond our natural into His supernatural—beyond our ordinary into His extraordinary—we can be sure that there are beautiful blessings connected to what He requires.

He doesn't ask those who are naturally animated to be still at times in order to hurt them, but to help them. He doesn't ask those who are given to war to aim for peace at times to hurt them, but to help them. He doesn't ask the timid to be bold at times to hurt them, but to help them.

It's all rooted in God's people being transformed into His likeness as awakened worshipers by approaching Him as He actually *is* instead of how we wish or imagine Him to be. In this way, we find ourselves coming beautifully before His throne with balance. With rejoicing *and* trembling. Intimacy *and* reverence. Vibrancy *and* stillness. Mourning *and* celebration.

CHAPTER 17

WITH EXTRAVAGANCE

"Rejoice in him and make a fool of yourself
for him the way lovers have always made
fools of themselves for the one they love."

—FREDERICK BUECHNER

MANY OF US are uncomfortable with worship of the extravagant kind. I was. Not sure exactly why. Okay, I might have a hunch. Pretty sure you do, too.

As stated in Chapter 14, it's ironic. We have no trouble worshiping other things with extravagance. Sports. Movie stars. Rock stars. Money. Food. Ideas. Success. Yada, yada, yada.

I didn't grow up worshiping God extravagantly. I mean, I worshiped Him. From my heart. And with my resources. Some of them. On Sundays and in youth group. But not so much outwardly. Extravagantly. Well, truthfully. Not so much inwardly. Extravagantly either. I don't think I knew how to awaken extravagant worship.

But I was determined to change that in my late twenties. I resolved to learn to worship God extravagantly. No matter the cost. I remember. Before my Sonicflood days. I resolved to become the worshiper I read about in the Bible. The David who said, *"I will not present burnt offerings that have cost me nothing!"* (1 Chron. 21:24). The Esther who stepped out in faith and declared, *"If I must die, I must die"*

(Esther 4:16). The Stephen who shouted as he was martyred, *"Lord, don't charge them with this sin!"* (Acts 7:60). The Paul who rebuked Peter in front of the other disciples for acting like a hypocrite (see Gal. 2:14). The Peter who stepped boldly out of the boat and onto the water, determined to get to Jesus (see Matt. 14:29). The blind beggar who wouldn't be silenced when he heard Jesus was nearby (see Luke 18:39). The Jacob who wrestled with God and wouldn't let go until He blessed him (see Gen. 32:26).

Story after story. The brave. The passionate. The desperate. The extravagant. And I—I entertained this crazy idea that these Bible heroes weren't especially privileged or different or better than me. But that I too could live out a passionate life of awakened worship, just as they did.

So, I made a plan. Rooted in God's Word. And in self-discipline.

WORSHIP WARFARE

I began waking up every day. A little earlier than before. To do three things. To read God's Word. To talk with Him. And to worship Him in song. It all intensified for me just after Martha and I first moved to Nashville in 1993.

I had grown up reading the Bible and praying in my time alone with God, but not worshiping Him with music. I knew this was where it needed to start. Not with one. Or two. But with all three. Like a three-strand cord that could not—that would not—be broken.

This is where David started. It's true. He didn't face Goliath or King Saul or the Philistines head-on because he was mighty in battle. No. He first grew mighty in another type of battle. Worship warfare.

It didn't even start with the lion or the bear. It started on the hilly pastures of Bethlehem. With the sheep. Where David lost himself in God. His Refuge. His Source. His Song. He learned to grow powerful in faith by hanging out with the God who made the lion and the bear—his Abba—in the secret place. The worship place. The relationship place. Why? Because David knew what all awakened worshipers know. *The secret to life is the secret place.*

That's how he was able to shout down Goliath:

> *You come to me with sword, spear, and javelin, but I come to you in the name of the Lord of Heaven's Armies—the God of the armies of Israel, whom you have defied. Today the Lord will conquer you, and I will kill you and cut off your head. And then I will give the dead bodies of your men to the birds and wild animals, and the whole world will know that there is a God in Israel! And everyone assembled here will know that the Lord rescues his people, but not with sword and spear. This is the Lord's battle, and he will give you to us!* (1 Samuel 17:45-47)

Woah. Intense.

I desperately coveted that type of authority in my walk with God. But how does a little scrawny teenager acquire such a radical God-confidence that he can speak in this manner to a full-on nine-foot-tall, mega-ginormous, totally insane battle ninja?

I'll tell you one thing. It doesn't start on the battlefield. And it doesn't start in basic combat training. No. We're talking about a different type of soldier.

It all starts with worship. Awakened worship warfare.

Yep. And that's how I was going to do it—to grow in extravagant love and trust for my Father, God. I would take my knowledge of the Word, my desire to be near Him, and my love for music and fuse them all together into a prevailing expression of worship that would inevitably defeat every giant in my life. Fear. Anger. Lust. Depression. Pride. Jealousy. Apathy. All of it.

And so, it began.

I took one look at my feet and spoke out loud: "Feet, it's time to dance. Hands, it's time to reach out. Knees, it's time to bow down. Voice, it's time to shout! To the King. With love. With passion. In triumph." Daily I would meet with God, seeking Him radically in relationship.

We had three tiny bedrooms in our first little home in Nashville. Over time—with daily surrender—I got to the point where I would crank up the music and dance all throughout the entire house, lifting my heart, my body, my mind, my soul, my face, my voice, and my life to the Creator without reservation. Without insecurity. With awakened extravagance.

This type of expression isn't cultivated overnight. It comes with years of consistent "practice." Years of denying our flesh. Paul said, *"I discipline my body like an athlete, training it to do what it should. Otherwise, I fear that after preaching to others I myself might be disqualified"* (1 Cor. 9:27).

I am still maturing in awakened worship warfare with each passing day. Even at age 48.

Funny. Many people see me in worship now and dismiss my exuberance toward God as simply a part of my personality. Ha! No. And yes! But not in the way you think. Not my natural personality. My supernatural personality! My new-hearted, new-natured, new-creation personality. The one where Jesus took over and crucified my original personality. So my old one is almost entirely gone, and His new one has almost entirely come!

Little did I know I was training myself—disciplining myself—for battles yet to come. For giants yet to come. For battles in the earthly realm. For giants in the spiritual realm.

You see, Kingdom victory does not lie simply in being smart or resourceful. In being skilled or optimistic. It lies in walking closely—intimately—with the One who is the source of all victory. Young David knew this. And I was learning it. Slowly. But surely. With each authentic prayer. Each transformational scripture. Each life-giving song.

LIKE SWEET PERFUME

It was a hot and sticky day, but one lady decided to worship—no matter what *they* would think. She made her way into an exclusive, high-powered meeting of some of the most powerful Christian leaders of the day. She didn't belong. She knew it. She didn't care. Able to evade security for the moment, she slipped in, right in the middle of their lavish dinner gathering.

Walking humbly—yet boldly—up to the unassuming man at the head of the table, she dropped to her knees and began weeping. Everyone froze. Stunned. What was happening? She wept for many reasons—some she understood and some she didn't. She wept for her sins. They were many. She wept for the highly influential, yet obviously hard-hearted power players in the room. They didn't understand who they were meeting with. She wept prophetically, for the man at the head of the table and the betrayal He would face. And she wept for the bystanders—the extras—the fans—who would ultimately be confused and shattered by it all.

Her tears cascaded directly onto His weary feet. He didn't move a muscle. For what seemed like forever. Then she did the unthinkable. She removed a priceless bottle of perfume from her bag and broke it, pouring it over Jesus' feet—and wiping them with her hair.

The owner of the place thought disparagingly to himself, "Ah. This proves it! He can't be from God. If He was, He would know. He would see the filthy woman who is touching him, and He'd throw her out in a New York second." Others protested, "It's an outrage. What a waste! Why not sell the perfume and offer the money to the homeless—the beggars." But Jesus sat quietly—taking it all in—humbly receiving her awakened worship.

He realized immediately, of course, that she was the only one in the room truly seeking Him. Truly loving Him. Truly worshiping Him. As He deserved. As He required.

Then He spoke. Sternly. He admonished some of the Christian leaders and then turned gently to the woman. Lovingly—yet with great authority—He forgave her and sent her on her way. In peace.

What was different about this woman? Why did Jesus respond to her this way? Why does the Bible record her story? Should we cheer her on? Should we attempt to imitate her approach? Clearly, we should. Jesus honored her and shared her story to spur us onward. Toward extravagant, unhindered, awakened worship.

Amazingly, this woman had already poignantly recognized what Jesus' brother, James, would write years later: *"Come close to God, and God will come close to you"* (James 4:8).

Was she perfect? Hardly. Was she sinless? Nope. Was she like us? In need of a Savior? You bet. Yet she didn't shrink back. She drew close. She pressed in. She cried out. To Jesus. Despite her shortcomings. Despite her insecurities. Despite the embarrassment. She didn't stay away or persist as a spectator. She didn't decline Jesus' invitation out of false humility.

She risked greatly. She didn't care what people thought. She went against every social norm. Heck, her reputation was ruined already. What did she have to lose? What do we?

She humbled herself. In repentance. On her knees with tears. She worshiped affectionately—some would say inappropriately—with kisses and caresses. But Jesus wasn't troubled. Not one bit. He didn't rebuke her. Or resist her. Or push her away. He forgave her. He had compassion on her. He received her.

How does this make us feel? How does this make *you* feel? Anxious? Embarrassed? Angry? Judged?

She gave it all. Relationally and financially. She loved deeply. She broke something open—something costly—in order to engage in relationship. With her Savior. With Jesus. She faced ruin, rejection, and humiliation. Yet she didn't blink. She was determined to become an extraordinary worshiper. An extravagant worshiper. An awakened worshiper.

So. Where do we stand? Are we willing to go there? To be all in? Or is this too much? Is there too much at stake? Too much to risk?

In the end, it is clear that there are three types of people in this story—three types of people reading this book. 1) Those outside looking in. The pre-saved. 2) Those present at the meeting—enjoying the aroma of the perfume—for a passing moment. Churchgoers. 3) And those fully engaged with Jesus. Next to Him. Touching Him. Hand in hand with Him. Soaked in the perfume of the Kingdom. God's true children.

It's true. There are those who *hear* about the story, those who *witness* the story, and those who actually *live* the story. Which are you?

Maybe we're contented with being present in the room, enjoying the waft of the perfume from a safe distance—around "nice services," "pleasant sermons," and "cheery songs"—when what we really need to do is walk out boldly and lovingly into this dying world completely drenched in perfume. In the aroma of Christ. With the scent of a nothing-quite-like-it God-friendship emanating fragrantly from our very souls.

Only two people walked out of that place with a serious dose of perfume on their person—Jesus and the woman. Everyone else played it safe. Everyone else enjoyed the scent for the moment, yet didn't lean in close enough to let it touch their skin—to let it come in direct contact with their soul. Everyone else watched from afar and, therefore, didn't absorb enough of the aroma to be noticed—to make a difference in the world—after they left the party.

Jesus is inviting us to break something open. To lean in closely. To get messy. No matter the tears. No matter the cost. No matter the potential loss. He is inviting us to fully embrace the fragrant scent of the Kingdom. To be rid of the putrid odor of the world. To become the extravagant worshipers He intends us to be.

> *Our lives are a Christ-like fragrance rising up to God. But this fragrance is perceived differently by those who are being saved and by those who are perishing. To those who are*

perishing, we are a dreadful smell of death and doom. But to those who are being saved, we are a life-giving perfume (2 Corinthians 2:15-16).

EMBARRASSED BY LOVE

What a song.

I remember hearing my close friend and mentee, Jonathan Lee, lead the song, "Pour My Love on You," at Pure Worship Institute (pureworship.org) a couple years ago. Wow.

> *Like oil upon your feet*
> *Like wine for you to drink*
> *Like water from my heart*
> *I pour my love on you*
> *If praise is like perfume*
> *I'll lavish mine on you*
> *Till every drop is gone*
> *I'll pour my love on you*

I wondered. Do we get embarrassed when we imagine the idea of loving on Jesus? On God? On the Holy Spirit?

I remember listening to a Scott Wesley Brown cassette when I was in middle school. Yes, a cassette lol. Back then, the idea of singing a love song to Jesus seemed offensive to me. Eeeww. I guess it was in the way I was raised. Or maybe it was just because I was a boy who liked sports, trucks, mud, worms, and stuff. You know. Boy stuff. (Sorry ladies. Don't be offended. It's okay if you like that stuff too.) Maybe I just had a harder time connecting—like many others—with the idea of being the Bride of Christ.

I definitely remember snickering the first time someone read from Song of Solomon. And the time after that. I didn't know how to process this style of love for God. It seemed odd—when referring to the Creator of the universe—to hear words like *lover* or phrases like *your love is sweeter than wine.* You can be sure I didn't want to hear about some lady's cheeks being like pomegranates or her neck being like the tower of David or her teeth being as white as sheep or her hair being like a flock of goats frisking down the slopes of Gilead. Yikes. And I definitely—beyond a shadow of a doubt—did not want to hear about her breasts being like clusters of grapes!

So, I giggled. It was the easiest way to get around having to decipher what it all meant. For me. For God. For the Church. For worship. Honestly, I had no idea this lovey-dovey Christianity was pertinent to me. To my walk with God. To awakened worship.

I was just embarrassed. One hundred percent.

But I was beginning to climb out of that pit. To explore. Maybe it was the foolish dancing and jumping—in my living room—that was helping me increase in my new, all-consuming love for God, which in turn was breaking the chains of dead religion off of me. Making me free. Like nothing else ever had.

Mikey tried it. Mikey liked it. And so, I decided to go full-on, lavishing my love upon the Father. Even if it killed me.

Funny thing. It was killing me. Killing me dead. Just like Paul said.

My old self has been crucified with Christ. It is no longer I who live, but Christ lives in me. So I live in this earthly body by trusting in the Son of God, who loved me and gave himself for me (Galatians 2:20).

MORE UNDIGNIFIED THAN THIS

Don't get me wrong. It wasn't solely the singing and dancing in my living room that was turning me into an extravagant worshiper. That's not it at all. But—like David—it was awakening something in me behind the scenes. Helping me develop into a true worshiper. A passionate worshiper. A bold worshiper. When no one was watching.

Interestingly, David was out in the fields becoming an awakened worshiper while his brothers were being considered for kingship.

David was out in the fields becoming an awakened worshiper while holding down the not-so-glamorous job of watching sheep. Ultimately, David was out in the fields becoming an awakened worshiper when no one was watching so that he wouldn't have to fake it when everyone was watching. When the lion and the bear attacked and everything was on the line. When Goliath held God's people in the grip of fear and nobody believed in this little juvenile. When King Saul hunted him down relentlessly—day after day—with a taste for blood. And when his own wife utterly despised him for it all.

> *But as the Ark of the Lord entered the City of David, Michal, the daughter of Saul, looked down from her window. When she saw King David leaping and dancing before the Lord, she was filled with contempt for him. ... When David returned home to bless his own family, Michal, the daughter of Saul, came out to meet him. She said in disgust, "How distinguished the king of Israel looked today, shamelessly exposing himself to the servant girls like any vulgar person might do!" David retorted to Michal, "I was dancing before the Lord, who chose me above your father and all his family! He appointed me as the leader of Israel, the people of the Lord, so I celebrate before the Lord. Yes, and I am willing to look even more foolish than this, even to be humiliated in my own eyes! But those servant girls you mentioned will indeed think I am distinguished!"*
> (2 Samuel 6:16, 20-22)

I love the way the New King James Version words it. *"And I will be even more undignified than this, and will be humble in my own sight"* (2 Sam. 6:22 NKJV).

He was unashamed of his extravagant worship. Recognizing—unlike Michal—that those watching his "ridiculous" expressions would be inspired, rather than offended, by his passion for God. Recognizing that his extravagant worship—while appalling and pride-filled to some—actually embodied humility in the eyes of the Lord. The only eyes that mattered.

Why? Because pride restrains us—keeps us from worshiping God extravagantly. Pride holds us in its formidable clutches, like a giant magnet, pulling, drawing, holding us captive. It is pride that reasons. That rationalizes. What will people think? What will people say? What will happen to my reputation?

All the while, it is humility that paves the road for you—for me—to develop into true "undignified" awakened worshipers.

Reflect on this.

> *Pride restrains us—keeps us from worshiping God extravagantly.*

> *Instead, God chose things the world considers foolish in order to shame those who think they are wise. And he chose things that are powerless to shame those who are powerful. God chose things despised by the world, things counted as nothing at all, and used them to bring to nothing what the world considers important* (1 Corinthians 1:27-28).

Living as Christ—in complete abandonment to our own desires—is foolishness to the world. Foolishness to the Pharisee. Foolishness to the 'wise.' Yet David was willing to appear foolish unto men in order to become wise unto God. Of course, God isn't asking us to become foolish. No. Yet often what He asks of us certainly appears foolish to those who are lost or who are consumed by dead religion.

Odd, isn't it? Which is more foolish? Dancing for men? Or dancing for God? Exalting God's creation? Or exalting the Creator of all things? Abandonment in sexual perversion? Or abandonment in worship? You decide.

> *And so, dear brothers and sisters, I plead with you to give your bodies to God because of all he has done for you. Let them be a living and holy sacrifice—the kind he will find acceptable. This is truly the way to worship him* (Romans 12:1).

CHAPTER 18

LIKE A CHILD

*"We are perishing for lack of wonder,
not for lack of wonders."*

–G.K. CHESTERTON

ISN'T IT FUNNY how we spend our entire young lives yearning to be adults only to find it works just the opposite in the Kingdom? It's strange. In God's economy, the supposed highest goal can end up being the lowest, while the assumed lowest ambition can end up being the highest?

I call it Reverse Godology—the Kingdom principle that exposes the Devil's cunning ploy to flip truth on its head. God's truth.

Think of it—if the enemy of our souls can get us thinking upside down, he can eventually get us to think of God as the problem rather than the solution.

Sound familiar? We see it every day in our "enlightened" world.

When we begin to believe that dark is light, that sweet is sour, and that good is evil, eventually we'll become earnestly indignant over seemingly foundational Kingdom fallacies.

Huh?

You know. We'll begin to believe the world's lie.

The same goes for our maturity in Christ. Some mistakenly assume that youthfulness inexorably equates to immaturity while old age and life experience always point to maturity.

Not so fast.

BORN AGAIN

Even as we grow older, Jesus implores us to remain young. Spiritually. This is one of the most notable characteristics of awakened pure worshipers. They become—or remain—childlike.

Interestingly, it all starts with being born again—becoming like a baby—something we would all rightfully resist if it actually meant doing so physically. Thankfully, as He invites Nicodemus to be born again in John 3:5, Jesus isn't referring to the physical realm. He's referring to the spiritual realm. To spiritual youth.

In Second Corinthians 4:16, we are encouraged by Paul to not lose heart. *"Though our [physical] bodies are dying, our spirits are being renewed every day,"* he states.

Despite this fact—that our physical bodies are growing older with each passing day—we will only persist in spiritual youthfulness to the degree that we remain united with the One who exists outside of time. Intriguingly, this is not only fascinating, but apparently it is also a matter of life and death.

Like us, the disciples were often childish in their attempts to understand the Kingdom. Competing. Vying for position. Jockeying.

In one such instance, Jesus was all but fed up with them as they argued about who was the best. Luke recalls Jesus' words, writing, *"Anyone who welcomes a little child like this on my behalf welcomes me, and anyone who welcomes me also welcomes my Father who sent me. Whoever is the least among you is the greatest"* (Luke 9:48).

Matthew's account of this same teaching adds the exclamation point: *"I tell you the truth, unless you turn from your sins and become like little children, you will never get into the Kingdom of Heaven. So anyone who becomes as humble as this little child is the greatest in the Kingdom of Heaven"* (Matt. 18:3-4).

Okay.

What is Jesus saying? How can He talk like this? After all, we've worked tirelessly to put aside our childish ways—to exchange diapers for dapper and adolescence for elegance—and now, suddenly Jesus pitches us the ultimate curve ball, demanding we return to childishness?

What gives?

Um, before we get too excited, let's discuss what it means to *become* like a child.

UNCOMMON FAITH

I always love the story of the feeding of the five thousand. You know, the one where the ordinary little boy offers his lunch to the Savior to feed the multitudes.

"Can you see it?" a preacher friend of mine laughed. "That little kid had to have been there that day—in the hungry mob—without his parents. Honestly, if his folks had been there on the hillside with him, we can assume his modest lunch would never have made it into the Master's hands."

No doubt. It takes great faith to offer such an insignificant remedy in attempt to provide such a significant solution to such a grand dilemma. Great faith. Uncommon faith. Awakened faith.

Think about it. Any ordinary parent would have shushed little "Johnny" at his offer to share his lunch. You can hear it now—my own paternal voice muttering, "Not so fast, Johnny. Your mother worked too hard putting together that lunch. If we simply give it to Jesus, there won't even be enough for our family, let alone the thousands of others around us. You understand. We shouldn't draw attention to the fact that we have food when others don't. We don't want to embarrass them. What difference could it make anyway? It will only complicate matters."

Man. Can you hear it? In *my* unyielding fatherly voice? In yours?

This illustration is nearly flawless. It serves as a powerful eye-opener concerning the typical response of the faithless adult. The adult Jesus is begging us not to become—in contrast to the faith-filled, awakened adult—the adult Jesus is empowering us to become.

The "rational" adult cannot see past the obvious reasoning of the situation, while the naive child is simply "irrational" enough to take the necessary steps of faith—to believe.

Don't misunderstand. I'm not suggesting the little boy was more spiritual and was therefore more capable of participating in the miracle at hand. No. It wasn't that he was *more* spiritual. It was that he wasn't *too* spiritual, *too* mature, *too* astute to believe. That he hadn't become so adultish that it neutered his ability to believe for the impossible. Gratefully, he wasn't yet ruined for the miraculous as many "proper" adults are.

> The naive child is simply "irrational" enough to take the necessary steps of faith—to believe.

Of course, this is a fairly weighty challenge for those of us who are increasing in years. Myself included. It is a serious enough issue that the Bible is not alone in its qualms. Many popular kids' movies highlight this plotline over and over again in attempt to aid people of all ages in avoiding the ever-increasing aptitude for failing belief characterized by so many adults.

CHILDLIKENESS OR CHILDISHNESS

Movies like *Peter Pan*, *The Chronicles of Narnia*, and *The Polar Express* reveal the beauty and mystery of rekindling our hearts for the unexplainable, the extravagant, the miraculous—even as we become *more* aware. Even as we grow *more* mature.

The film *The Chronicles of Narnia: Prince Caspian*, based on C.S. Lewis' book, depicts a scenario where the older children are beginning to wane in their ability to see Aslan, the Lion—the Christ-like figure in the movie. Sadly, only the youngest, Lucy, seems to have maintained her ability to see him, whereas before, each child was capable of this magical association.

The main character in *The Polar Express* movie, Chris, has seemingly lost his belief in Santa Claus. His faded faith is symbolized in his inability to hear the jingle of the silver bells adorning Santa's reindeer. No matter how they shake and wiggle, Chris just can't seem to hear them.

Ironic. Both tales paint a picture of eyes that can't see and ears that can't hear. Whether there is an intentional spiritual connection or not, this is precisely what begins to happen to scores of adults as they "mature." Their spiritual eyes and ears gradually, naturally stop functioning. Growing numb to the wondrous things of God—often as a result of life's pain, struggles, or disappointments. Scales cover their eyes and ears so that the still small voice of the Lion of the Tribe of Judah grows ever distant.

So, what *does* it look like to come as a child? To worship as a child?

First, we must understand the grand distinction between becoming childish and becoming childlike. These two are nowhere near the same universe. In fact, they are sheer opposites.

When we think of childish, we think of tantrums, bickering over toys, refusing to eat vegetables, whining over unfair treatment. Pretty much primal selfishness. That place where the whole world revolves around me. Myself. And I.

This, of course, is not what Jesus is after.

He is after the beautiful, uncapped vitality of His innocent ones— the dreamers, the hopefuls, the singers, the dancers, the builders, and the lovers. Think of the best characteristics of little children. They don't hide behind political correctness. They call things as they are. They aren't worried about food or shelter. It never crosses their minds to wonder if they will have enough. They aren't concerned about race or cultural differences—status or social hierarchy. Shoot, my kids aren't even concerned about knowing the names of potential playmates. Their sole concern? That a person be breathing and willing to share in an adventure.

THE DNA OF AN AWAKENED WORSHIPER

Take another look at Matthew 18:3-4: *"I tell you the truth, unless you turn from your sins and become like little children, you will never get into the Kingdom of Heaven. So anyone who becomes as humble as this little child is the greatest in the Kingdom of Heaven."*

Clearly, there are two primary truths at play—both of which have bearing on access to the Kingdom of Heaven. First, that we must turn from our sins, and second, that we must become like little children.

We all know Jesus is the only way to the Father, yet we discover here that part of what it means to come to the Father—what it means to become like Jesus—is being willing to repent of sin. Yet of seemingly similar importance is *being willing to become—or remain—like a little child.* These two appear to be joined at the hip.

Obviously, God is not asking us to become something Jesus is not. So we can gather from this passage—and others—that Jesus has, of course, forsaken sin completely and that He also embodies what it means to become like a child. Hopefully this doesn't wreak havoc on your Jesus-theology.

We know. Jesus is humble while others are prideful. Jesus speaks up while others are silent. Jesus is silent while others complain. Jesus reaches a His hand out while others stick their noses up. Jesus receives little children while others turn them away. Jesus lets go of His life while others hold on to theirs.

To be like Jesus. That is what it means to come as a child. To be one with the Father. This is what it means to be born again. To be transformed into a new creation. To be spiritually young. This is what it means to worship with awakened abandonment. Not with reticence. To worship with delight. Not with disgust. To worship in freedom. Not in cynicism. To worship because we get to. Not because we have to. This is the party we've been invited to. This is the DNA of an awakened worshiper.

Are you free? Am I? Or are we constantly worried about what others think? Are we optimistic, or are we the ultimate Eeyore— Winnie the Pooh's gloomy little friend? Are we too cool for school, or are we too blessed to be depressed? (Sorry.) Are we fully trusting in Christ, or are we fully overcome by fear?

There is no entrance into God's Kingdom without childlike faith. This much is clear. We must allow Jesus to strip us of our pompous self-righteousness. Our arrogant cynicism. And our dangerous disbelief. All while allowing Him to awaken us to childlike worship. To do what He does best. Set us—the captives—free!

> *There is no entrance into God's Kingdom without childlike faith.*

He is inviting us to become like Him—like a child. Carefree. Hopeful. Kind. Merciful. Forgiving. Possibly even a bit naive. Thankfully, He hasn't left us on our own but has provided the means for us to do so—through His blood, through repentance, and through the power of His Spirit.

CHAPTER 19

WHEN WE DON'T FEEL LIKE IT

"If you only do what you feel like doing, you are not a believer, you are a feeler."
—BILL JOHNSON

DID YOU EVER do something you didn't feel like doing only to discover later you were incredibly grateful you did it?

Piano lessons were like that for me. As each Monday evening rolled around, I dreaded going. It wasn't like I didn't practice or wanted to quit, but as a young middle-schooler, I could always find 25 other things I'd rather be doing.

I'd slip sulkily into my mom's car and moan about how much I didn't want to go. Funny thing. While I was there, I played well and really enjoyed it. My teacher was cool and very encouraging. I always left feeling like a million bucks.

Until the next Monday. And we'd do the whole thing all over again.

Every week was the same. Until I finally wised up. One day I thought to myself, "Come on, Jeff. Why whine and complain every week about your lesson when you really like playing and are actually pretty good at it? It makes no sense! So...stop it!" And I did.

We do this with God too. Don't we? And with church. And with worship.

I've found it happens a lot.

Exercise is like this. I hate exercising with a perfect passion, but of course, I typically feel energized afterward and am fairly stoked that I made the sacrifice. How about apologies? We avoid them like the plague, but if we can ever get the nerve up to utter the words, "Please forgive me," it's like the weight of all the world is lifted.

EARLY THE NEXT MORNING

Abraham understood our plight better than most. If you recall, he had an assignment he wasn't too thrilled about—from the Maker himself. An assignment devised for a would-be awakened worshiper. Genesis 22 lays it out.

God approaches His servant, Abraham, and resolves to test him by instructing him to take his one and only son, Isaac, the son of promise, the one he loved so deeply, his one and only son, capable of carrying on the family name—yep, that's the one—and sacrifice him as an offering unto God, Himself. Sounds exhilarating.

Seriously? And I thought my troubles were bad! I can't even fathom how I would feel if God asked me to do something this outlandish. Take my firstborn, Roman, out back and slaughter him? Wow. That's excruciating to consider. Especially without the privilege of knowing the end of the story.

And yet astonishingly, the Bible recalls that early the next morning, Abraham got up, saddled his donkey, called for his two servants and his son, and started up the arduous mountain road. To worship.

A few years ago, a good friend of ours reached out to us about some uneasy feelings he was having. Yep, after 25 years of marriage, three kids, a couple cats and a dog or three, he was ready to call it quits. Unfortunately, he'd made some poor choices and was now facing an increasingly broken marriage. And he was done. Just done.

As he shared his story, I'll never forget his distressing words. "Jeff and Martha, I just don't love her anymore. And I don't want to be fake. I don't know what to do. I can't stay with her if I don't have feelings for her, right?"

My first thought? Wow. So noble. This guy wants to be real. Authentic. He is clearly refusing to fake the funk with something as serious as covenantal love. He wants to be true to his feelings. How honorable.

Wait a minute. Not so fast.

FEELINGS RULE, ACTIONS DROOL

There's a growing misconception—in our mega-enlightened world—that *feelings precede actions*. Isn't that how it works? We wait to act on something until we feel like acting? And if we don't feel like it, we just don't do it. We've come to accept this as normal. And as a result, we are essentially ruled by our feelings. Our cravings. We consume what we crave. No questions asked.

If we have a hankering for a McDonald's cheeseburger, we eat one. Likewise, if we don't have a taste for broccoli, we reason broccoli's just not for us. Yet, we disregard a very important point in the process. Fact is, God wired us just the opposite—*with a natural bent toward craving what we consume rather than consuming what we crave.*

> We were actually designed to construct our cravings by first choosing what we consume.

Yes, it's true.

This is something I initially learned from author and speaker John Bevere. It just doesn't work the way we think. We don't consume what we crave. No. We were actually designed to construct our cravings by first choosing what we consume. This is the way God made us. Not to follow or obey our feelings, but to create and nurture them.

If I wait until I feel like getting out of bed, I imagine I'll never stop hitting the snooze. If I wait until I feel like eating my veggies, I'll likely resort to chicken fingers and ranch dressing for every meal. And if I wait until I feel like praying, I'll likely surf the heavenly airwaves only in a crisis.

Believe it or not, scientific studies prove people can proactively change their taste toward food—their likes and dislikes—by what they choose to eat and not eat. We've all seen it. Kids who don't like certain foods have their palates altered by being "forced" to eat things they initially didn't enjoy. To their delight!

Really? Can we actually tweak our taste buds?

Sure. Isn't this a common understanding with things like alcohol and coffee? The acquired taste? Where we develop a taste for things only after choosing to consume them consistently over time? Few folks enjoy their first beer or cup of black coffee, but with a little determination, a craving—even an addiction—can easily be cultivated. What if we applied this principle on a grander scale, but for the good?

TEST OF OUR FAITH

Honestly, I grow weary of hearing people say, "Nah, I don't eat rabbit food. Salad just doesn't agree with me." Really? Interesting. Many hold erroneously to the idea that their dislike of vegetables justifies not eating them. But what if—just maybe—the issue is not taste at all? What if the reason we *don't* like to eat our greens is simply because we *won't* eat our greens? What if the truth is that parents around the world have deprived their children of maturing their taste buds simply because they don't want to make their kids "suffer" by eating a celery stick? (Which, I admit, can be challenging to choke down without peanut butter or guacamole.)

What if by taking action—to do something that is not a natural desire—we discover we can actually transform our natural desires?

Most people say they have to believe it to see it, but truth is, faith works the other way around. If we want to see it, we have to believe it. Action always comes first. Believing before seeing.

Remember our Bill Johnson quote at the top of the chapter? "If you only do what you feel like doing, you are not a believer, you are a feeler." This is what separates true believers in Jesus from unbelievers.

Do we imagine under any circumstances that Abraham *felt* like sacrificing Isaac? Do we imagine it was part of his natural disposition? Killing his one and only son? Of course not. In fact, that was the point. He had to completely disregard his feelings to prove he had faith. He had to put feet to his faith to prove that his faith was real—to God *and* to himself. To prove that his faith and trust in God were not based solely on empty emotion. See, it's one thing to say we have faith, but we don't really know for sure until our faith is put to the test?

The angel of God said to Abraham, "Now, I know that you truly fear God."

But don't miss this. Equally important was the fact that Abraham discovered this about himself as well. How did he discover it? Because actions speak louder than words. And actions produce change in our cravings that build character.

Take my friend. Though his words about his wife seemed respectable—in an odd sort of way—he had it all backwards. That particular night was actually when I first started pondering this issue. I remember hearing the Holy Spirit whisper to me the very counsel I gave to him—that I now share with you.

"Love is not a feeling. Love is a decision. Isn't this how you kindled the relationship with your wife in the first place? Sure, you had an initial attraction, but you took action and began cultivating love for her in the form of date nights, gifts, tender 'I love yous,' and late night marathon phone conversations. Isn't it possible the reason you don't have feelings for your wife now is not because you somehow magically lost your original attraction, but because you stopped cultivating it?"

Graham Kendrick's words get right to the heart of the issue: "Worship has been misunderstood as something that arises from a feeling which 'comes upon you,' but it is vital that we understand it is rooted in a conscious act of the will."

People don't just wake up 25 years into marriage and say, "Wow, look at us—not sure how we ended up with a loving relationship. Must have been that rabbit's foot!" No. It takes work. Commitment. Dedication. Selflessness. And perseverance.

I continued. "Just think. If you were to go home and, by faith, begin doing the things you did when you first fell in love. You would absolutely—without a doubt—begin to awaken your love for your wife all over again. Why? Because feelings don't precede actions. Actions precede feelings, and feelings follow actions."

It's the same with our relationship with God. When we lose that goose-bumpy feeling toward His Word or His presence, we don't just shrug our shoulders and say, "Oh well, what's a guy to do?" No. We start doing the things we initially did to stir up those emotions. To stir up REALationship. To awaken pure worship.

C.S. Lewis says it this way in *Mere Christianity*, "When you are behaving as if you love someone [including God], you will presently come to love them."

Boom.

FAITH IT TO MAKE IT

"But Jeff, I don't want to be fake!" Great! Then don't be. Don't fake it to make it. Faith it to make it.

Ever notice? Just when you don't feel like praying—if you'll step out and pray anyway, time has a way of turning seconds into minutes into hours—even before you know it? Same thing can be said about musical worship. Rarely do I automatically jump for joy when someone says, "Hey guys, let's get together and worship God for a couple hours!" But as I step out in faith to sing, to lift my hands, to focus my mind on giving God glory, something shifts. My emotions toward God are stirred. My actions—taken in faith, apart from my feelings—stir up genuine emotions and true love for God. And I find myself passionately participating in the very thing I had little desire for initially.

Matt Redman, worship leader and songwriter of the song "The Heart of Worship," testifies to this very thing; "So often when my worship has dried up, it's because I haven't been fueling the fire. I haven't set aside any time to soak myself under the showers of God's revelation. Often, time is the key factor. But if we can find space to soak ourselves in God's Word, his presence, his creation and spend time with other believers, then we'll find that the revelation floods back into our lives; and our hearts will respond with a blaze of worship once more."

Jesus replied, "I am the bread of life. Whoever comes to me will never be hungry again. Whoever believes in me will never be thirsty" (John 6:35).

Reading God's Word is like a feast for our souls, but many of us simply haven't developed a taste for it. We say, "It's boring," or "I just don't understand it." All the while, we have proactively awakened a commanding appetite for the things of the world. We must realize. There is great joy and tremendous spiritual nourishment to be had if we will simply consume God's Word by faith instead of waiting for the impromptu rise of our feelings. When we learn to treasure God's Word by faith, it awakens to us as we begin to nurture our true hunger for it.

An added bonus? Our appetite for this world certainly decreases as we spend less and less time consuming it.

The same goes for awakening our appetite for time spent worshiping God in song. When we don't feel like worshiping Him—that's the best time to start. Just like our friends, Paul and Silas.

SOMETIME AROUND MIDNIGHT

You know the story.

Paul and Silas were beaten and thrown into prison for casting a demon out of a fortune-telling slave girl. Wild stuff. She was trailing them day after day as they journeyed to the place of prayer, shouting, *"These men are servants of the Most High God, and they have come to tell you how to be saved"* (Acts 16:17).

Thanks, Captain Obvious.

Exasperated, Paul finally turned to the woman and commanded the demon to come out of her—which it promptly did. This put everyone into a tizzy because this one young lady earned loads of cash for her masters by telling peoples' fortunes. A mob quickly formed, and like I mentioned, Paul and Silas were placed in prison after being stripped and beaten with wooden rods.

Not a good day.

There they lay—bruised and bleeding—in the middle of the inner dungeon, with their feet clamped in stocks. Not only were they in terrible pain, but they were locked down tight in an extremely uncomfortable position. With no hope of escape.

Perfect.

If there was ever a time for mortified moaning about the ministry or revved-up "why me" ranting about service to God or desperate dysfunction concerning one's desire for death, this was it.

Nevertheless, sometime around midnight, Paul and Silas decided to strike up the band. To sing a few cheery choruses. Right there in the middle of hell. With aching bones, open wounds, and iron stocks on their feet. Come on. If there ever was a time to *not* feel like singing, this was it.

But I guess that's the point. Because, as they sang, miracles started happening. Big ones. Real ones. Not as an inspiration *for* their singing, mind you, but as a *result* of their singing.

With every prisoner eavesdropping—there in the dark—these boys lifted their baritone voices in worship to the Most High God. Not questioning His wisdom in allowing them to suffer, but exalting His matchless name for the whole, wide world to hear.

Just then, a violent earthquake shook the place. Chains fell off. Of every prisoner. Doors burst open. Throughout the whole institution.

The jailer pulled out his sword to commit suicide—fearing the worst—but Paul yelled out, letting him know everyone was still there. What happened next? Just as you expected. The jailer and his entire family gave their hearts to Christ. They fed Paul and Silas and washed their wounds. And this—this radical, didn't-feel-like-worshiping awakened worship—paved the way for them to walk away scot-free.

You may have noticed. They didn't wait until they felt like worshiping, but they worshiped right in the middle of their darkest hour—right in front of those who despised them—right in the moment when no one else in their right mind would ever do such a thing!

But, isn't that what Matthew 6:21 is getting at? *"For where your treasure is, there your heart will be also"* (NIV). Most folks assume it's our heart that directs us toward what we should treasure, but the truth is the reverse. In order to awaken my heart toward a treasure—toward something truly worth treasuring—I must first begin to treasure it *by faith*. Then and then only will I find my heart treasuring what it should treasure. A true treasure.

This is the essence of faith. This is the essence of the Kingdom.

How do we worship God when we don't feel like it? How do we forgive those who so deeply wound us? How do we die to self? How do we maintain peace in our hearts in the midst of great chaos? By feelings? No. By faith. And whatever we do in faith will certainly, eventually awaken true and genuine emotions that will flow supernaturally out of our beings.

Truth is, if we wait until we stop feeling afraid, we will always be afraid. If we wait until we stop feeling depressed, we will always

If we declare our courage in the face of the fear and champion our God-given purpose in the face of the depression, we will overcome by the blood of the Lamb and the power of the Holy Spirit.

be depressed. But if we declare our courage in the face of the fear and champion our God-given purpose in the face of the depression, we will overcome by the blood of the Lamb and the power of the Holy Spirit. Awakened worshipers worship wholeheartedly even when the songs aren't right, the lights aren't perfect, the singers aren't on pitch, and the feelings aren't there. They worship by faith, and this makes all the difference.

CHAPTER 20

WITH GREAT BIG GOD PERSPECTIVE

"If God were small enough to be understood, He would not be big enough to be worshiped."
—Evelyn Underhill

I STARTED THINKING recently. About how unbelievably massive God must be. I mean, seriously. How big is He? How big is big? Is He merely spiritually big, or is He also physically big? Does the term *mighty* sum Him up? How about *majestic*? *Gargantuan*? Still, what do these words even mean when considering God's infinite power and endless magnitude?

Somebody get a thesaurus!

When you think of our Creator, how "awesome" do you picture Him? I guess I'm just the kind of guy who wants to know. Both for myself and because, as a worship leader—or any other kind of Kingdom leader—I recognize part of my responsibility is helping point people to our amazing…um…gigantic…uh…colossal God.

I admit. I actually sit around thinking about ways to do just that. Whether through songs or prayers or scriptures. Or silence. I scour the Bible for samples—for keys—that could possibly help us grasp God's magnitude. In real and tangible ways. Mostly to silence my flesh and the lying tongues of this modern age. Seems as though every worldly voice is cunningly working overtime attempting to stuff our monumental God into a neat little box. One we can understand. Which is understandable. Kind of.

I've noticed. There are others doing the same as me. My friend Francis Chan spoke at Passion 2017 and astonished the crowd of 70,000-plus with his thoughts of what it all means—how terrifying it is—that we can actually approach the God of all gods. In person. In prayer. And He listens!

He explained. "I'm literally going to talk to Him—and He created the heavens. And He's going to hear me. He's going to listen to me. You guys, this is the most amazing opportunity—that we get to speak to God."

After reading from Hebrews 12, he continued. "We're going to come into His presence now. This blazing fire. And when He spoke back then, it was like the people were asking Him not to speak anymore, because they couldn't take His voice. And yet I'm going to speak to Him right now." Then he fell on his knees and invited everyone to join him in praying to this unfathomable God. Our God.

Chan's preaching slot at Passion 2017 occurred following a real-time satellite call with a real-life NASA astronaut. Yet—as awesome as this was—Chan took the opportunity to remind the gatherers that speaking with God is eternally more important and infinitely more astonishing than speaking even with a modern-day space traveler.

I wondered. Why did he feel the need to do this? Maybe because we are so easily amazed by everything else. Except God. He recognized our great potential to become more enamored with man than with God. And he realized this singular issue has more potential to erode awakened relationship with God than most other issues combined.

It's true. I find—if I'm not careful—I easily grow indifferent to God's beauty and greatness. Especially when I allow myself to marvel at man's beauty and greatness. Even the words we use to describe

Him quickly lose their punch. I am keenly aware of the battle. There-fore, I will not—I cannot—allow it to overpower me. No. I resist with every fiber of my being in the power of the Spirit in order to keep God firmly reigning on the throne of my heart.

HE OWNS IT ALL

One of the greatest weapons I've found to aid me in right-sizing my God is what I call "big God" scriptures. Here are a couple I turn to when my heart needs a little defibrillation.

Psalm 50. This entire passage—which I referenced for a different reason in Chapter 7—helps breathe new life into our understanding of God, revealing hidden and often forgotten parts of who He is. Here in these verse—through Asaph—He unveils one of His very foundational characteristics.

> *But I do not need the bulls from your barns or the goats from your pens. For all the animals of the forest are mine, and I own the cattle on a thousand hills. I know every bird on the mountains, and all the animals of the field are mine* (Psalm 50:9-11).

To me, there is endless grandeur in these words.

What do we learn exactly? Simply that God has no needs. For bulls. For sacrifice. For sustenance. For anything, really. But we also learn that the entire world is His—as well as everything in it. *Every-thing.* He owns it all. And there is no other being who shares this ownership with Him. Not the angels. Not the demons. Not the devil. And certainly not His people.

He owns each and every galaxy. He holds the titles to the stars. He claims each leaf on every tree on every hillside over the entire globe. As well as the globe itself.

He breathed life into the first animal and into every single one since. He owns the sky, the seas, the air, and the land. Strangely, we imagine sometimes that we own the property our homes sit on—even as we buy and sell it—but technically, truthfully we don't. God is simply lending it to us for now. It is His. And we are stewards of all He owns (see Lev. 25:23).

We've all uttered these words: "That's mine!" But truthfully, we cannot say these words, because we truly do not own anything. Not one blade of grass. Not one hair on our heads. My skin isn't mine. My thumbnail isn't mine. My iPhone isn't mine. My car isn't mine (even though it's paid off). My heart isn't mine. The blood running through my veins isn't mine. My nose hairs aren't mine. (Sorry.) Even my own kids aren't mine.

Psalm 95:4-5 screams, *"He holds in his hands the depths of the earth and the mightiest mountains. The sea belongs to him, for he made it. His hands formed the dry land, too."* What? While you and I are squabbling over petty things, God is talking about owning mountains and oceans, asteroids and planets, and even the furthest reaches of the universe itself.

Great. Big. God.

I spent nine years as a kid living in Colorado, and I've visited often since my parents moved back. My family loves the Rocky Mountains. There's nothing like climbing to the top of a 14,000-foot massive mound of boulders, looking out over the endless sea of snow-capped, pointy peaks, and breathing in the clear, crisp air—God's air—as you take in the beauty of it all.

I've never tried to count the peaks, but from where I've stood I'm sure I couldn't number even one percent of all the peaks in the world. Yet if God were standing beside me, He would point to the tall, jagged one over there past that little lake—*His* lake—and say, "Yeah, I own that one. And the one behind it…it's mine, too. And the one way over there beyond those clouds…and that other one you can barely see. Yeah, it's mine, too. They're all mine." And for Him, it is actually entirely true. You get the point.

I wonder. Is it possible we may have *slightly* underestimated God? Maybe?

Sort of?

Great. Big. God.

LIKE WAX BEFORE HIM

Psalm 97:3-4 declares, *"Fire spreads ahead of him and burns up all his foes. His lightning flashes out across the world. The earth sees and trembles. The mountains melt like wax before the Lord."* Jeremiah 10:14 stresses that, compared to Him, *"The whole human race is foolish and has no knowledge!"* Psalm 33:7 says, *"He assigned the sea its boundaries and locked the oceans in vast reservoirs."* Isaiah 40:22 tells us that it is God who sits above the circle of the earth, and that all the people below must seem like grasshoppers to Him!

In Isaiah 40:25, God asks, *"To whom will you compare me? Who is my equal?"* He continues. *"Look up into the heavens. Who created all the stars? He brings them out like an army, one after another, calling each by its name. Because of his great power and incomparable strength, not a single one is missing"* (Isaiah 40:26).

Great. Big. God.

Have you seen the stars recently? No, seriously. Have you gone outside and actually gazed up at the stars? On a crystal-clear night. Away from the city? Recently? There are billions of them within each galaxy and billions of galaxies within the universe. The *known* universe, that is. And the Bible goes on to say that God measures the universe with His fingers (see Isa. 40:12). Stretch out your hand. Can you or I even span the full diameter of a basketball? I mean, thinking of God in these terms—with hands that are that big—imagine if He approached the earth in all His fullness. By the time He got within a billion miles, all we would see are the pores in His skin.

Great. Big. God.

Isaiah 46:9-10 reminds us that God even knows the future. *"Remember the things I have done in the past. For I alone am God! I am*

God, and there is none like me. Only I can tell you the future before it even happens. Everything I plan will come to pass, for I do whatever I wish."

Hmmm, maybe we have *grossly* underestimated God. Yes. I'm pretty sure we have. In fact, I think there are times when I imagine in my ignorance that God is only a little bit bigger than I am. A little bit taller. A little bit smarter. A little bit more experienced. I mean, I know things, right?

We are just grasshoppers, people. Our lives are but dust. Every breath is a gift. Every beat of our heart is allowed only by the astounding mercy of God. Psalm 50:22 even explains that God will tear us apart if we ignore Him—yikes.

Great. Big. God.

No wonder the Bible says the Israelites trembled and quaked when God was coming down from the mountain to speak to them. Exodus 19:16-18 records it:

> *On the morning of the third day, thunder roared and lightning flashed, and a dense cloud came down on the mountain. There was a long, loud blast from a ram's horn, and all the people trembled. Moses led them out from the camp to meet with God, and they stood at the foot of the mountain. All of Mount Sinai was covered with smoke because the Lord had descended on it in the form of fire. The smoke billowed into the sky like smoke from a brick kiln, and the whole mountain shook violently.*

Can you picture it? Sounds ridiculous, doesn't it? Or does it? Maybe we've grown numb. Maybe we've seen too many incredible movie special effects—CGI—to truly be astounded by something as lackluster as God.

Remember. When Moses asked to see God's glory in Exodus 33, God told him this was impossible. Why? Think about this. Because to peer directly at the face of God would mean certain and immediate death. Certain. Immediate. Death.

What?

Now, that's power, my friend. I mean, if God were to fully—and comprehensively—disclose Himself to any human being, they/we would not survive the encounter. It would result in our instantaneous demise. Why? Because He is a consuming fire (see Heb. 12:29). He is not *like* a consuming fire. He *is* a consuming fire.

Let that sink in.

Great. Big. God.

TERRIBLE GOD

How does all of this great big God stuff help us awaken worship? Think of how Daniel responded when the angel came to visit him in Daniel 10. He fainted twice. His strength left him, and his face grew deathly pale. He lay there with his face to the ground, as dead. Then, after the angel touched him and lifted him, he stood, yet he could not keep from trembling—knees knocking, lips quivering, heart pounding.

And this was only an *angel*. Merely one of God's messengers!

Warning. Big, whopping statement coming.

If we never find ourselves falling before God, the reality is we've never truly encountered Him!

It's crazy. We struggle to worship. We yawn. We shift in our chairs. We're tired after three minutes of singing. Our minds wander, and we can't wait to get back to the things that truly inspire us.

But wait. If we are uninspired by God, maybe we've yet to actually encounter Him. Maybe we've yet to bump into Him. The One whose gaze can kill. Literally. The One who causes the mountains to leap like a young bull. The One whose voice twists mighty oaks and strips the forests bare.

I mean, if we *had* bumped into Him, we would have known it. Right? And we could not have left unchanged. If we had encountered

> *If we never find ourselves falling before God, the reality is we've never truly encountered Him!*

Him, we would have been so completely rocked by the meeting that we could never have looked at Him—at His Word, at His Kingdom—the same ever again. We would never again allow ourselves to sit passively in the musical worship portion of our services, drinking our coffee and watching the clock. The fact that we do these things proves we have not encountered Him. As He has desired.

Read through the horrifying chapters of Job 38-39. God thunders at Job and his friends.

> *Have you ever commanded the morning to appear and caused the dawn to rise in the east? Have you made the daylight spread to the ends of the earth to bring an end to the night's wickedness? ...Do you know where the gates of death are located? Have you seen the gates of utter gloom? Do you realize the extent of the earth? Tell me about it if you know! ...Can you direct the movement of the stars— binding the cluster of the Pleiades or loosening the cords of Orion? Can you direct the constellations through the seasons or guide the Bear with her cubs across the heavens?* (Job 38:12-13,17-18,31-32)

Great. Big. God.

So now what? Well, for starters, we need to increase our reverence, honor, and veneration toward God.

But how? Gritting our teeth and trying harder than before? No. Making grander promises to God—vowing to finally worship Him the way he deserves? No. It's simple. We ask. Ask God to help us. Help us shift our perspective. Help us break out of the numb. Help us to see Him. Truly. With spiritual eyes. In a way we've never imagined. In truth and in spirit.

Just ask.

And then determine to be willing and obedient to do whatever He says in response to our asking. By faith. And in the power of the Holy Spirit.

Truth be told. We may seriously need to repent over how we've dishonored Him. Yes, repent. He is greatly honored when we respond in repentance—by humbling ourselves in His presence. It shows that we understand our place as well as His place. When we humble ourselves, it opens the door for God to reveal Himself in ways we were closed off to Him before.

It would even be fitting to allow ourselves to tremble a little bit—or a lot a bit—at His immensity and splendor. His beauty and magnificence. Not with a forced reverence, but in response to an invitation. Yes. *Because awakened worship is not an obligation but an invitation.* To come close. To see Him. To know Him as He is. As terrifying and wonderful as this may be. We want to return the favor by inviting Him to stir up the fear of the Lord in our lives. Once and for all. Via supernatural revelation from His Word and from His Spirit.

It's frustrating. And scary. But it's easy to let words like *marvelous, wonderful, spectacular, majestic,* and *holy* lose their oomph. Why? Because we've used them without really knowing what we're saying. Or because we've used them casually to describe pizza.

FIGHTING DESENSITIZATION

Trust me. It's not merely that our words have lost their meaning, and it's undoubtedly not that God's glory has diminished in any way. It's either that we have failed to thirst for who He really is or that we have allowed ourselves to become desensitized to His immeasurable greatness as a result of our fascination with the things of *His* creation. Plain and simple.

Are there other ways to fight God-desensitization? To awaken pure worship? Besides stirring up extravagant worship? Besides becoming like a child? Besides worshiping when we don't feel like it? Besides meditating on big-God scriptures?

Sure there are.

You knew it was coming, didn't you?

Here it is. Again.

Spending time alone with God—communing, abiding, fellowshipping, seeking, meditating—is, of course, absolutely the most effective way for us to increase our capacity to see Him as He is. (Of course, we won't see Him perfectly this side of heaven, but hopefully we'll be on the path to seeing Him more and more, not less and less.)

Did you see that word back there? *Increase.* Yep. Spending time with God greatly increases our ability to see Him. Just as not spending time with Him slowly decreases our ability to see Him—by slowly fastening thicker and thicker scales upon our spiritual eyes. Surely, we didn't think we would grow closer to God by spending less time with Him, right?

Of course, keeping the magnificence of God before us is not so much about understanding the facts. It's not simply about knowing or quoting what's true. Anyone can do that. It's about keeping our hearts alive. Toward those facts. About God. Toward the beauty of who God is. Toward friendship with Him. And realizing our tendency to grow complacent. To grow calloused. To grow indifferent. Toward God. And refusing to allow this to happen. Come hell or high water.

I don't want to unknowingly slip into a pool of lukewarm soup. The place where meditating on God doesn't terrify *and* electrify me any longer. The place where fellowshipping with God doesn't fill me with joy *and* with fear any longer.

This reminds me of something I learned, of all things, from the movie *Rio.* Have you seen it? Remember the scene where Rafael takes Jewel and Blu, who are handcuffed together, to meet his friend—the large, drooling pit bull, Luiz? (You gotta look up this scene on YouTube.) They walk into a dark and spooky garage while some subtle, ominous music plays.

Wait. This can't be right! Could this possibly be the place Rafael had promised, where the two soon-to-be love birds would have their cuffs removed?

Out of nowhere, Luiz explodes from the shadows, barking and pursuing the birds—who begin fleeing for their lives with a seemingly well-rehearsed three-legged running style. Luiz pounces on the two macaws and then stops just short of devouring them. What he says next is perfect. And it helps us better understand the fear of the Lord.

With paws pressing the frightened birds to the floor and drool hanging as low as it possibly can without licking their faces, Luiz suddenly changes his predacious expression and quips, "I gots yous good!" (Cue the nauseating sound of drool being sucked up.) He continues. "I coulda ripped your throats out, but I didn't!" Then he pauses. Thinks. And says, curiously, "But, I coulda."

How does this help us understand the fear of the Lord?

Easy.

We may not like it, but at any moment God has the power to squash us like little gnats on a window screen. He brought us into this world, and He can certainly bring us out—if He wants to. Whenever He wants to.

Don't get me wrong. It's not like God is running around terrorizing us by saying things like, "I could have squashed you guys like tiny little bugs. But I didn't. Yet." No. That's not the point.

The point is we should hold in our hearts a constant attitude of humility, as if God *could* be saying this. Even though He is not. But He could. No, not in the sense that we should imagine at any second He might actually squash us, but in the sense that we understand His power to be so formidable, that He would be able to destroy us easily if He chose to. Yet, instead, He has promised to love us.

Great. Big. God.

He is greater in power than we could ever imagine. And we are completely vulnerable to Him. Yet He has made a covenant with us to guide and shepherd us carefully. Just as Luiz guides the two macaws.

Yep, Luiz never threatens the birds again. In fact, he helps them and protects them from their greatest enemies. Yet the unstated truth remains—he could take them out if he so chose.

This is the fear of the Lord. And the fear of the Lord helps us remain awakened to how utterly magnanimous God is. Realizing this truth. That God is incredibly scary—because of His unequaled power—yet that He is infinitely more loving than He is scary. The fact is, it is really scary just how loving He is!

Thank goodness for perspective.

In addition to God being bigger and more powerful and more outrageous than we could ever fathom, He is also more tender-hearted, more caring, and more compassionate. And His patience extends further than we ever dreamed. His generosity is immeasurable. His faithfulness is unbounded. He is literally overflowing with gentleness and exploding with graciousness. His friendship is without compromise, and His incredible love is truly and absolutely unfailing.

Oh, how great are God's riches and wisdom and knowledge! How impossible it is for us to understand his decisions and his ways! For who can know the Lord's thoughts? Who knows enough to give him advice? And who has given him so much that he needs to pay it back? For everything comes from him and exists by his power and is intended for his glory. All glory to him forever! Amen (Romans 11:33-36).

Oh, yeah. He's a great big God, and it is impossible for us to ever, ever overestimate His glory. Even if we try, we will utterly fail. And that's a good thing. A really good thing. Francis Chan reminds us, "Isn't it a comfort to worship a God we cannot exaggerate?"

So, go for it. Try to overstate His enormity. Go on. Overexaggerate His faithfulness. Tell a "fish story" about how wonderful He is. Double dog dare ya. Try to make Him sound more wonderful than He really is. Bet you can't.

CHAPTER 21

FACE TO FACE

"This quest for his face is the ultimate quest. But to embrace the quest for the face of God, one must be ready to die."

—BILL JOHNSON

THIS IS MY heart's desire. To awaken face-to-face pure worship. In me. In us. In our families. In my church. In *the* Church. In our neighborhoods. In our hometowns. In our cities. In the United States of America. And in this broken world.

What does this mean? Well, to me it has something to do with music—because music is a uniquely powerful, God-crafted tool designed to aid us in stepping out into real-time communication with our heavenly Father.

But awakening pure worship is much more than music, too. I've shared it throughout this book, and I'll share it again—one more time—in this final chapter. Just in case.

When we are awakened to pure worship—when pure worship is allowed to spring to life within us—it means we are learning and yearning to be with God in our secret, private lives as well as in our visible, public lives. It's where we find ourselves regularly communicating with Him quietly, deep in our hearts, as well as boldly, out in the open—establishing a new normal where we anticipate God's involvement in all of our moments. In everyone's moments. All throughout the day. Each day.

When pure worship is allowed to awaken in us, we notice ourselves moving away from a flailing *I have to* mentality toward a flourishing *I get to* mentality. We reject our former, skewed perspective that somehow brands church, Bible study, musical worship, prayer, and obedience as a burdensome obligation to rules and tradition rather than as an extraordinary invitation to love and friendship.

But it's not for the faint at heart. Awakened pure worship, that is. Every force on earth and in hell is coming against us. True relationship with God is just too dangerous to be allowed to go unchecked. There is too much at stake. For the kingdom of darkness.

It's nuts. Living this type of life is absolutely the easiest *and* most difficult thing you will ever do. It involves a major perspective shift. A serious paradigm shift. And a massive priority shift. The kind of shift that happens when we truly believe that a God-brewed relationship is both possible and available. For every beating heart. For every breathing soul.

THE AFTER GLOW

Most of us know the story of Moses and his fantastic glowing face. Incredibly, he would spend time with God inside the Tent of Meeting and would come out with his face literally radiant from having been in God's presence.

Seriously?

> *Moses remained there on the mountain with the Lord forty days and forty nights. In all that time he ate no bread and drank no water. And the Lord wrote the terms of the cove-nant—the Ten Commandments—on the stone tablets. When Moses came down Mount Sinai carrying the two stone tablets inscribed with the terms of the covenant, he wasn't aware that his face had become radiant because he*

*had spoken to the Lord. So when Aaron and the people of
Israel saw the radiance of Moses' face, they were afraid to
come near him* (Exodus 34:28-30).

That is crazy cool.

Yet we can easily miss the point if we focus on the wonder of the
glow rather than the reason for the glow. What is the point? Not that
Moses' face glowed. No. The point was this—that while Moses was
up on that mountain, he was "with the Lord." Yes. With the Lord.
Those three words. With the Lord. *This* is why his face was radiant.
Not because he was special. *This* is why his face glowed. Because he
met *with* God. Face to face. As friends.

And *this* is exactly how God wants to meet with you. Face to face.
Check it out!

*Inside the Tent of Meeting, the Lord would speak to Moses
face to face, as one speaks to a friend* (Exodus 33:11).

Huh? Is this possible? For me? As one speaks to a friend? With
God? Wait. You mean to tell me this guy was hanging out with
Almighty God? As friends do? Chilling with the Lord? Face to Face?
Yes. In ways that many of us cannot truly fathom. Sadly. But in ways
that God has made available for all of us to enjoy.

KISSING THE FACE OF GOD

One of the Greek words for worship—*proskuneo*—literally means to
kiss the hand or face of God in the same way a dog would affectionately lick his master's hand or face.[1] Seem odd? Maybe. But let's
push beyond our normal reservations for once. What exactly is taking place—best-case scenario—when man's best friend licks his
master's hands or face? He does so with reverence, friendship, submission, playfulness, and love, all wrapped into one. Right? And his
master does not pull away in disgust. No. He welcomes the expression of genuine—and often sloppy—love and friendship, probably

while down on one knee, looking his companion in the eye. A sincere friendship that cannot be explained with words.

This is how God is with us. He sees as us the apple of His eye.

Keep me as the apple of your eye; hide me in the shadow of your wings (Psalm 17:8 NIV).

The phrase *apple of my eye* refers to something or someone cherished above everything else. So, could it be that God cherishes you—and me—above all other aspects of His creation? Yes, of course He does. This is His heart. This is our reality as children of God. All by design.

I've heard it said that there's something more to this *apple of my eye* expression. Something that goes beyond the obvious definition. Have you ever looked deep into someone's eyes and stared? Have you ever gotten close enough to see something you would never have seen if you hadn't gotten that close? Uncomfortably close? If you have, you might know already what I'm about to say. (No, not eye boogers.) Something much different. A reflection. Of yourself. In the apple or center of the other person's eye.

Try it. It's pretty rad.

This is exactly what God sees when He looks at us—when we venture close enough to kiss His face or look Him in the eye. He sees Himself. His own reflection. In you. In the apple of your eye. As you allow Him to gaze lovingly back at you—like a good, good Father—straight through you, to the eyes of your heart. What a powerful reminder that we are fearfully and wonderfully made. In His image.

I really love what this reveals about God, but I love even more what it reveals about us. Think about it. It's just not natural to be so bold as to look God right in the eye. At least not for very long. If someone looks us right in the eye a little too long, we typically turn away. Honestly, many of us have a hard time looking people in the eye at all. Let alone God.

We are so insecure. So full of shame. So overwhelmed with fear. That our head and eyes fall automatically to the floor to avoid the possibility of God—or anyone else—seeing us for who we really are.

But this is not God's heart. No way. (He can already see who we are, anyway.) And yet, He is calling us to lock eyes with Him. Face to face. In REALationship. Not so He can peer into our eyes and see how wretched we are. But so we can peer into His eyes and see how wonderful He is.

Amazingly, when we find ourselves unafraid to look God directly in the eye, it reveals something sensational. That we have begun to embrace a truer understanding of who we really are in Christ. That we have begun to cultivate a healthy, awakened relationship between us. That our shame has been erased by the blood of Jesus. That we have finally settled somewhere deep in our heart that we are actually children of God. His sons. His daughters.

Question. When you look God directly in the eye, what do you see staring back at you? His love? His patience? His compassion? Or His anger, His rules, and His displeasure. I see His strong, soft eyes and His inviting, proud smile. Why? Because I'm good? No. Because He is.

This perspective changes everything.

When my eyes are locked with my Creator's, I avoid becoming sidetracked by worldly ideas that leave me proud, depressed, and entitled. I avoid becoming consumed with feelings of isolation, fear, and anxiety. I avoid buying into the lies of hopelessness, rage, and misdirection. I cling to what He says about me. Every word.

But be warned. It is often these lying emotions that keep us from drawing close enough to God to meet with Him face to face from the start. Thankfully, this is exactly what Jesus' blood has done. Vanquished the voices and leveled the lies so we can truly—and finally—walk in close fellowship with our God. Think of it this way. Jesus didn't die for your sins. He died to bring you back into face-to-face fellowship with God, and your sins were just standing in the way!

FACE FIRST

Knowing how to approach God in worship—with extravagance, like a child, when we don't feel like it, and with great big God perspective—means understanding the priority of seeking His face over seeking His hands. Here me out. The metaphor of seeking His hands speaks to the act of seeking God's blessings and His gifts, His miracles and His provision, His rewards and His power. But the metaphor of seeking His face speaks to the act of approaching God simply for who He is. For His person. For His friendship. For REALationship.

Interestingly, there are many little hints throughout Scripture that clue us in to the fact that God—like us—prefers face-first seeking over hands-first seeking. This is fairly standard fare in relationships, is it not? If my children continually come to me only for what I can give them—money, keys to the car, help with homework, food for their stomachs—we won't have much basis for a fruitful relationship. Of course. Healthy relationships are always built on the foundation of love and openness, trust and transparency.

Likewise, Psalm 103:7 makes an important distinction when it comes to the difference between God's relationship with Moses and His relationship with the people of Israel. *"He revealed his character to Moses and his deeds to the people of Israel."* This difference is subtle, but it is important enough to note.

It is truly incredible that God would choose to reveal anything of Himself to anyone. So, as expected, it is not a complete letdown when David speaks of God's willingness to reveal His deeds to the people of Israel. Even so, if we were forced to make a choice between God revealing His character—who He is—versus God revealing His deeds—what He's done—it certainly wouldn't take much thought to decipher which of the two tells of richer relationship.

The things God has done for us are too wonderful for words. But the revelation of His deeds alone cannot usher us into closer proximity with His person. His deeds do reveal how He cares for us. But they do not cultivate in and of themselves greater closeness with Him. To Him.

How beautiful is it then that Psalm 103:7 speaks of God revealing His character to Moses! Now, we're talking about all the barriers being removed. About the fences and the boundaries being stripped away. Now, we're speaking of close proximity. True transparency. And true intimacy.

Did you notice? God opened His heart to Moses—the one who sought to meet with Him face to face. But God did not open His heart in the same way to the Israelites—the ones who chose to stay back, to remain at a safe distance. The ones who chose to let Moses speak to God on their behalf rather than venture close enough to look Him in the eye (see Exod. 19 and 20).

MORE THAN MANSIONS

I've been walking this journey with God for 44 years—ever since I received Christ when I was four. I have grown exponentially, especially as it has to do with understanding face-to-face encounters with God. And still, I feel as though I have only scratched the surface considering the full extent of the available riches of God's friendship.

After 17 years of life in Nashville as a traveling artist and worship leader, God called me out in 2010 to begin reproducing myself by pouring into the hearts and lives of the students at North Central University. We've been working hard to ignite a culture of awakened pure worship in our God-drenched school, divinely positioned in the heart of downtown Minneapolis, Minnesota. And it has been incredible to see the growth over the last eight years as many have moved from survival mode to revival mode. And we're just getting started!

So, which are you? One who stands at a distance and lets the preacher chase a deeper walk with God on your behalf? Or one who is willing to risk everything to get close? Close enough to awaken pure worship?

What about it? Are you willing to accept the biblical premise that our principal passion in life should not be to fulfill our dreams, our desires, or our pleasures? That our primary purpose should not be realized in our education, our status, our likes, or our position?

What if the purpose of heaven was not primarily to see the pearly gates, walk the streets of gold, or dance on the crystal sea? What if it isn't first and foremost to admire that fancy crown, tour that impressive mansion, or even take that glorious new body for a spin? What if it isn't even to have our tears wiped away, our pain whisked away, or to be reunited with all our loved ones?

What if the primary reason for your existence—for mine—is simply to be with God? All together?

Would you be okay with that? Would I?

What if the whole point of going through all the wild journeys in this life is to do whatever it takes to get to the place where we are back in the garden—enjoying the new Jerusalem on a freshly fashioned planet Earth—hanging out with God? Laughing, sharing stories, and shooting the breeze? Exploring universes together?

Would that get your adrenaline pumping?

What if it really isn't so much about religious rules or church attendance after all? Or wearing the right clothes, having the right color carpet, or whether our church has a choir or not? What if it isn't primarily about miracles, or entertaining angels, or boasting about the number of people who've prayed the sinner's prayer in our services? Or how often we take communion, or whether we use the King James Version of the Bible or not?

Crazy as this sounds, what if it isn't even about hearing those infamous words; "Well done, my good and faithful servant?"

I mean, is that it? Is that the culmination of a life lived unto God? The great reward? A simple pat on the back and a "job well done" from our Master? Along with an eternal "see ya later"?

Certainly not!

Trust me. These words are going to be wonderful to hear, but this is not why we fight the good fight. This is not why we persevere in the face of great hardship and trial. This is not why we battle for our loved ones and cry out to God in the midnight hour. This is not why we repent with tears for the sins we commit or why we stand up for the marginalized and the oppressed.

Only to hear these words? I don't think so! Don't get me wrong. Lord willing, these undeserved gems will echo in our ears like the tongues of a billion angels, but to finally arrive on the shores of heaven certainly brings with it a much sweeter joy. Not merely the *words* of our Savior, but the astounding beauty of His countenance and the wonder of face-to-face fellowship with Him. To finally come together with our Lord in REALationship. In His actual, physical presence!

It will be overwhelming. So much so that we won't even notice crowns, mansions, or golden streets. Glassy seas, pearly gates, or other heavenly beings. It will be utterly beyond our comprehension. To stand—or fall—before Him. And then to jump up into His arms. To finally be there, reconciled to God. Restored. Fully. Truly. Wonderfully. Through the blood of Jesus in the power of the Holy Spirit.

This is what will make it all worthwhile. Lasting relationship. This is the prize. This is the pearl of great price. This is the eternal reward given to those who diligently seek Him. Love. This is what will afford complete satisfaction for our souls. Forever friendship. This is what will give eternity its radiance, its joy, and its utter fulfillment. Intimate fellowship. There will be no words to describe it. When we are once and for all reunited with the Maker of our soul. The Lover of our soul. Forever. Face to face. With God.

Is this something that might interest you?

It's definitely what interests God.

You.

The question is. How will I respond? How will you? To His invitation?

It won't be a walk in the park. There's too much at stake. There are too many distractors. Too many deceivers. Too many tempters. To many lukewarmers. No doubt. It'll be a battle. For your soul. For mine. So, we must go together. Stay together. Stick together. If we are to respond properly.

Yes. My hope beyond hope is that we will each respond in the same manner David did. *"My heart has heard you say, 'Come and talk with me.' And my heart responds, 'Lord, I am coming'"* (Ps. 27:8).

We accept your invitation, Father. Awaken pure worship in us. We are coming.

NOTE

1.   "Language Studies," s.v. proskuneo, Strong's #1834, Studylight.org, https://www.studylight.org/language-studies/greek-thoughts.html ?article=80.

ABOUT JEFF DEYO

JEFF DEYO IS a guy who believes in something. Something he knows will change your life. Something he knows will literally touch each and every corner of your world, from the practical to the relational to the emotional to the spiritual. Something simple that will actually make you a better father. A better wife. A better entrepreneur. A better daughter. A better lover. A better friend. And a better follower of Christ. Something small that will have a massive impact on you as a person. Taking you from sitting on the sidelines wishing you were diligent in the things of God to one who is actually becoming diligent in the things of God.

That thing?

TIME WITH GOD.

- What if he told you that by spending only 1 hour a day of focused, intimate time alone with your heavenly Father, you could add hours and weeks to your life and to your calendar?

- What if he told you that by putting God first in your life—above growing your social media following, climbing the corporate ladder, or even attempting to change the world—you could walk in peace, fulfillment, and ultimately in the abundant life Jesus promises? All with one tiny decision?

WOULD IT BE WORTH IT?

The ultimate question is, who do you want to be? There are many voices. There are many paths. Only you can choose. Jeff is simply echoing the voice of your Father in heaven—inviting you into the one thing you were created for—close fellowship with God. The one thing from which all the other things are born.

- He is not offering you a problem free life.

- He is not offering you success or fame.

- He is not offering you a plan to fulfill your greatest hopes and dreams.

He's offering you the one thing that touches the soul deeper than any other thing. Real, unadulterated connection with God. Real joy. Real hope. Real life. Something that inevitably will grant you the greatest possible gift in life—to know that you know that you know the Lord.

THIS IS AWAKENING PURE WORSHIP.

Join Jeff on the ride of your life.

Please visit jeffdeyo.com to gain access to multiple free downloads that will help you awaken pure worship in your life.